PASSING FOR BLACK

PASSING

FOR BLACK

The Life and Careers of

MAE STREET KIDD

Wade Hall

THE UNIVERSITY PRESS OF KENTUCKY

Publication of this volume was made possible in part by a grant
from the National Endowment for the Humanities.

Editorial and Sales Offices: The University Press of Kentucky
663 South Limestone Street, Lexington, Kentucky 40508-4008

01 00 99 98 97   1 2 3 4 5

Library of Congress Cataloging-in-Publication Data

Hall, Wade H.
     Passing for Black : the life and careers of Mae Street Kidd / Wade
Hall.
        p.   cm.
     Includes bibliographical references and index.
     ISBN 0-8131-1996-0 (acid-free paper)
     1. Kidd, Mae Street, 1904- . 2. Racially mixed people—
Kentucky—Biography. 3. Afro-American women legislators—Kentucky—
Biography. 4. Kentucky. General Assembly—Biography. 5. Afro-
Americans—Kentucky—History—20th century.   6. Kentucky—Race
relations. 7. Louisville (Ky.)—Biography. I. Kidd, Mae Street,
1904- . II. Title.
E185.97.K44H35 1997
976.9'04'092
[B]—DC20   96-23193

This book is printed on acid-free recycled paper
meeting the requirements of the American National Standard
for Permanence of Paper for Printed Library Materials.

Contents

Illustrations

Preface

This is the story of Mae Street Kidd, an African-American woman born in 1904 in Millersburg, Kentucky, a small town near Lexington, to a black mother and a white father. She has lived through—indeed, she is a living representation of—much of American history. Although she and her father lived within a few miles of each other, they never met. In fact, she never even saw him until she was grown and living in Louisville. One day, while Mae was visiting her mother, Anna Belle, in Millersburg, someone pointed him out in the post office. They did not speak. Throughout Anna Belle's long life (she died in 1984 at the age of 101), she never mentioned Mae's father to her, although she was reared with his name.

Minnie Mae Jones was raised by her mother and stepfather, attended the local black school, then spent two years at the Berea College–sponsored Lincoln Institute in Simpsonville, a boarding school for blacks from Kentucky counties with limited educational facilities for them. When she was twenty-one years old, she moved to Louisville as a single woman and became a successful businesswoman with the black owned and operated Mammoth Life Insurance Company. During World War II she served in England with the American Red Cross. Later she held jobs with United Seamen's Service in Portland, Maine, and with insurance and cosmetics companies in Chicago and Detroit. She was twice married and twice widowed. She has no children.

Well into her sixties, she became a politician, serving for seventeen years in the Kentucky General Assembly, where she crusaded successfully for open and low-income housing. Her most important symbolic achievement was sponsorship of a 1976 legislative resolution ratifying the Thirteenth, Fourteenth, and Fifteenth amendments to the U.S. Constitution, which freed the slaves and gave them the rights of citizenship, thus closing at last a dark chapter in Kentucky history.

Her achievements as a professional woman and politician are all the more remarkable when one realizes her limited formal education, her lack of family influence and support, her color, and her sex. As a Kentucky woman of color during a pioneer period of minority and women's rights, she has lived a fulfilled life through sheer will power, hard work, single-minded determination, and a belief that she could do anything she wanted. Throughout her business, professional, and public careers, she pursued her goals with fierce independence. She insisted on living her life her way. As one governor of Kentucky put it, "You don't play with Mae Street Kidd, and she doesn't play with you."

I wish to thank several people who have helped me to bring this book to print. First and foremost, I thank my good friend Gregg Swem, who painstakingly transcribed our taped interviews and made my work easy. I also thank Dr. Ernest Ellison, a retired dentist and professor of dentistry who is also a master photographer. He made copies of the precious photographs in Mrs. Kidd's scrapbooks. Finally, I thank the gracious and hospitable people in Millersburg who welcomed several strangers from Louisville to their town on Memorial Day 1995 and shared with us the present and past of their charming town: Linda Roozen of Main Street Antiques; Jimmy Pruitt, the local undertaker who knows where all the bodies are buried, living and deceased; and Mr. Craycraft, who showed us the site of Shipptown, where little Minnie Mae Jones grew up.

This self-narrative, based principally on some forty hours of taped interviews in the kitchen of Mrs. Kidd's home on Chestnut Street in Louisville in the spring of 1993, is an attempt to capture the voice and the spirit as well as the careers of Mae Street Kidd. No one, of course, speaks a book, no matter how eloquent she is. My job as author has been first to tap Mae Street Kidd's memories and opinions of people, places, and incidents, then to check newspapers and such standard references as *The Kentucky Encyclopedia* for factual accuracy, and finally to put it all together in a coherent narrative that captures her life and her language. As these pages will show, even after a debilitating stroke, heart attack, and loss of vision, Minnie Mae Jones Street Kidd's spirit and spunk are alive and well.

In her official capacity as state representative in 1977, Mrs. Kidd wrote to the pastor of her own church, Plymouth Congregational, congratulating the church on its centennial. In the letter she gave her definition of history, emphasizing its human dimension. "History," she wrote, "is more than a succession of dates and events, of crisis and controversy. It is illuminated, at its best, by the acts and words of the participants." Now, almost twenty years later, she will tell of her role in history—her own acts in her own words. Before, however, she speaks, let us make a short visit to the little rural Bluegrass town where her life began.

A Visit to Millersburg

To get to Millersburg, Kentucky, it's best to start from Lexington, taking the Paris Pike (Highway 68 north). Drive leisurely up the lovely two-lane, tree and rock-fence bordered road for a dozen miles to Paris, the seat of Bourbon County, circle the courthouse, then continue north for some six more miles. After you cross Hinkston Creek, you are in Millersburg.

Along this scenic route—one of the most beautiful in Kentucky—you will pass long rows of maples, pin oaks, and fir trees that line driveways leading back to old and new country mansions that befit a country bred to the sport of kings. In this heart of the Bluegrass it is easy to separate the owners of new minifarms from the old landed gentry. The names alone will do it: The Grange, Elmhurst, White Hall, and Claiborne are weathered by time and tradition, while Pleasure Acres, Bourbon Hills, Maplewood, and Breezy Heights have new-paint sparkle and luxury.

Here is a country of gently undulating grasslands of fescue and bluegrass—a green wonderland punctuated by small tobacco patches, blackened barns, fish ponds, and creosoted fences, which are replacing the more expensive whitewashed fences of yesterday. Thirteen miles west of Paris is Georgetown, a sleepy college town that was awakened to new life in 1987, when Toyota planted a huge automobile assembly plant nearby, remaking the countryside with dozens of new victorian-looking subdivisions and reinventing the economy with high-paying blue collar jobs and generous benefits. Whether old or new, a spread of five hundred acres or a baby farm of five acres, the home of a horse breeding dynasty or a two-bedroom starter house—every home seems picture-perfect, with a neatly manicured expanse of lawn and pasture. Despite the changes wrought by manufacturing and commerce, it is still a landscape where the progress of the seasons is marked by the careful cultivation of tobacco from spring planting to winter sales.

Paris is the seat of Bourbon County, formed in 1785 as one of nine counties by the Virginia legislature before Kentucky became a state in 1792. In a burst of Francophile fervor, fanned by France's support of the American Revolution, Kentuckians named many of their new towns and counties in honor of their ally, ranging from Louisville and La Grange to Versailles, Fayette, and Bourbon. For more than two hundred years it has been the heart of the garden of Kentucky, with its rich, productive soil of clay and limestone that produced abundances of corn, wheat, and hemp—a crop formerly used in making rope but now outlawed as a recreational smoke.

But we have come to Millersburg. Named long ago for its largest landowner, it seems oddly distant from the hustle and bustle going on in its neighboring towns. The traffic is heavy on Highway 68 as it shoots straight through the town, but not much of it stops to spend the night. Indeed, with a population of less than one thousand, it has hardly grown since its founding in 1817. In years past many of Kentucky's first families sent their sons and daughters to its two prestigious prep schools, Millersburg Military Institute and Millersburg Female College. Now only MMI, as it is called locally, remains, and it has adjusted to the new realities of the waning twentieth century. Indeed, Millersburg seems to have accepted its laid-back, let-well-enough-alone reputation. It honors its past with neatly kept old homes, a "historic district" of stone row houses, and tourist-seeking antiques shops that line the highway through town. The newer residents live in white frame houses with bonneted ceramic geese on yards and porches and in mobile

homes that stand where accidental fires cleared the ground.
The people are friendly and informed. They will show you
the town square with its ornate iron fence, where light opera
and other chautauqua events were held each summer under
a large tent. They will tell you stories about local people and
places that go well into the early years of the twentieth century and even reach back to the Civil War and slavery times.
They will offer you a glass of iced tea and show you the black
and white churches and take you to the town cemeteries where
prominent citizens of both races are buried some half a dozen
blocks from the town center.

They will take you across the bridge over Hinkston Creek
and over a washed-out road about a mile from town to
Shippsville or Shipptown, as it was sometimes called, where
early in this century almost fifty black families lived on land
deeded them by a former slave-owner named Shipp. It is the
birthplace of a woman of color—80 percent white and 20 percent black and Indian—born to a white father and a legally
black mother. As a girl she was called Minnie Mae Jones. As a
young woman of twenty-one, she took the L&N train (the
tracks are still there) south through Paris to Lexington and on
to Louisville, where she became a successful businesswoman
and politician named Mae Street Kidd. Shipptown has been
reclaimed by the weeds, bushes, and trees of neglect. Only an
occasional shard remains—a piece of pottery, a weathered
board, the fragment of a high-laced shoe—of a lively community struggling to survive in the shadow of slavery and poverty.

Before you leave Millersburg, you return to Vimont Street,
where little Mae Jones grew up after her mother bought a comfortable frame house across the street from the "colored" Methodist church. The house burned a few years ago, and in its
place is a trailer parked under a maple old enough to have
shaded the little girl as she played with the make-believe playmate she called Helen. The last places you stop are the cemeteries—first the white cemetery, where Mae Street Kidd's

Location of childhood home in Millersburg, Ky.

father, Charles Robert Jones (February 6, 1875–March 15, 1972) lies buried next to his wife, Leila MacClintock Jones (May 4, 1875–September 2, 1965), and one of their two daughters, Elizabeth Jones McCulloch (September 6, 1908–May 9, 1991). His younger daughter, Katherine Jones, lives about a block away.

Finally, you are taken around to the back side and through rusted barbed wire into another cemetery and to the grave sites of Mae Street Kidd's mother, brother, and stepfather. Her brother, George William Jones (July 18, 1901–July 6, 1986), lies next to his daughter Christine Jones, who died at the age of eight in 1929. Her stepfather, James W. (Willie) Taylor (1881–1959), is buried on a gentle slope under a silver maple tree next to her beloved mother, Anna Belle Leer (Jones) Taylor (1883–1984). It is time now to leave the tragedies and ironies of history and to utter a benediction in the words of Kentucky poet Allen Tate, who, like Mae Street Kidd, was born in the shadow of the Civil War in 1899 some twenty-five miles south in Winchester:

Graves of mother, stepfather, and niece in the "black" cemetery.

Leave now
The shut gate and the decomposing wall:
The gentle serpent, green in the mulberry bush,
Riots with his tongue through the hush—
Sentinel of the grave who counts us all!

And it is time to return to Louisville, to 2308 West Chestnut Street, where Mae Street Kidd waits to tell her story.

Introducing Mae Street Kidd

I was born on February 8, 1904, in the middle of a dark period for black people. Throughout the South the racial reforms and advances that had been made possible by the Civil War and Reconstruction had been mostly wiped out by racist politicians, aided and abetted by racists all over the country. In Kentucky 1904 was the year that the infamous Day Law took effect, which prohibited the mixing of races in both public and private schools. Many blacks lived in horror of lynching for minor and imaginary offenses. It seemed that the freed slaves and their children had once again been enslaved. I was born with the added burden of being more than 80 percent white and thus did not fit well into either black or white society. Legally, I was a Negro. Culturally and racially, I lived in a no-man's-land where I was discriminated against by members of both races. But I have survived with my dignity and honor intact. Not only have I survived but I have also managed to live a productive and joyful life.

Unfortunately, most of my work and joy is in the past. As I talk it's the spring of 1993, and I'm an old and disabled woman. I get tired easily. I am twice widowed. I've had a serious stroke, and I'm legally blind. You don't know what it means to sit here and look at a blank piece of paper. Oh, if I only had the use of one eye! Yes, if I had only one eye I could drive my car. I could write. I could read. I would never be lonesome. I am sometimes an angry and bitter and sad woman. I'm trying very hard, but there are times when I can hardly endure it. I have claustrophobia, and I fear being shut up in this house. One day recently I lost my keys and couldn't get out. I almost fainted. I was about to break a window when I finally located my keys and let myself out.

Sometimes I want to scream and complain to God about my pitiful state. I have always been an independent woman with a mind of my own, and now I have to depend upon other people. My stroke has turned my life upside down. I'm frustrated and disappointed, and I'm having to teach myself to put all that behind me and learn to live with what I have left. I wanted to write my life down in a book by myself, but now I can't do it. I can't drive my car. I have trouble getting around even in my own home. I can't go up and down the stairs by myself anymore, but I still know this house like the palm of my hand, every nook and cranny. I wish I could see it the way I used to.

My mind is a little cloudy now and my voice is not clear, but I still enjoy talking and I'll try to recall the people and events that make up my life. When my memory stumbles, I can check my two large scrapbooks full of newspaper and magazine clippings and other memorabilia that document my life. A friend called me a couple of weeks ago and said, "Mae, why don't you get somebody to help you write the story of your life. You've done too much for people not to know." I have asked Dr. Wade Hall of Bellarmine College to help me shape my life into a book. He will jog my memory with questions and take down my words. Then he will make it into a book that I hope will represent who I am. I want people to know that I've lived a good and valuable and significant life. I want this book to tell people I did something aside from being almost white. I don't mind my white blood—it's an important part of who I am—but what's more important is what I did with my life.

These scrapbooks testify to the life I've lived. Here is a picture of my blessed mother, a picture of me when I was six years old, a picture of me during my freshman year in the Kentucky General Assembly, and there are pictures of me with

During interviews with Wade Hall, 1993

people like Vice President Humphrey and Arthur Ashe and
Maynard Jackson and Julian Bond and several Kentucky governors. Here's a photograph of me with Governor Wendell
Ford, inscribed to me as "a worker for people." This is an invi-
tation from Mrs. Carter to a reception at the White House in
1979. Here's a clipping that says, "Rep. Kidd named state co-
chair for Sloane's gubernatorial campaign." Oh, these pictures
and clippings bring back such rich memories of my abundant
life! Indeed, I have been blessed with so much success; yet I
am still angry and frustrated. No memories can lighten the
darkness that imprisons me now! I can distinguish day from
night, light from dark, but that's not good enough. I don't want
sympathy, and I don't want you to tell me I'm doing all right.
People try to console me by saying, "Now Mae, you know that
there are a lot of people who are a lot worse off than you are."

I say, "To hell with that! Don't tell me that rubbish. I don't want to hear it." So you see that it is very hard for me to learn acceptance. I am trying to become more mellow, but it's not my nature to be inactive and passive.

I am trying to learn what God's will is for me now because, you see, I have always believed that I was one of His chosen people. Otherwise, I can't explain my life. Of course, He created all of us at birth, but I believe that some of us are chosen as precious vessels in whom He takes a special interest. I always felt that someone was out there watching over me, guiding me, helping me, urging me to move on up. I don't mean to brag, but I have risen to positions above people with better backgrounds and connections and more education. I have been called the lady of many careers. I was a successful salesman and executive with several insurance companies and a cosmetics company. I served my country overseas during World War II with the Red Cross. I have volunteered for many worthwhile community projects, and I served in the state legislature for almost twenty years. Yes, I believe that God has been guiding me. I believe that He has worked through other people to give me opportunities. They have noticed me and said, "Here's a woman who can do things and go places. Let's give her a little push." What they did was show me the door of opportunity and I opened it. Surely God has been with me all the years of my life, and surely He is telling me something now in my affliction. It has to mean something.

I am sitting on a high stool in my kitchen at my home at 2308 West Chestnut Street in Louisville, Kentucky. I have lived here for almost fifty years. I am proud of this house, my yard and flowers, my garage and the car inside it—a car which I can no longer drive. I am sitting on this stool because it's very comfortable for me in my crippled condition. The back of the chair supports my back. I'm a very tall woman and my feet can touch the floor. As you can see, my kitchen is spotless, even though I have to pay someone else to clean it for me now. A clean kitchen is something I learned from my mother.

With Vice President Hubert Humphrey

Presenting Arthur Ashe with a commission as a Kentucky Colonel

With Julian Bond and
Sam Robinson

Perhaps I should first tell you something about my physical and personal make-up. I am almost six feet tall, very tall for a woman. In my earlier years I was considered very beautiful, with fair skin and blonde hair. Tall, stately people are natural leaders. That's why I knew Ross Perot would never become president. He's too little! People tell me that everything stops and everyone notices me when I walk into a room, though I've never intentionally displayed myself. I don't court people with put-ons. With me, what you see is what you get. Take it or leave it because it's the real me. I have always behaved naturally. I've always walked with my shoulders back and my head up. My mother taught me as a young girl to be proud of myself. She said, "Mae, don't ever slump. Walk erect and show off your height. Let people *see* who you are."

After you've seen me and talked with me for a few minutes, you'll soon know that I have a mind of my own. You'll learn that I can't be controlled by other people. You'll see that I am polite and friendly to people, but I don't overdo it. I'm not gushy and sentimental and insincere. I don't hug and carry on over people falsely. When I say I like something or someone, it's genuine. Indeed, I take care of myself. I am a fanatic about cleanliness. I love beautiful clothes and hats. I think highly of myself, but I'm not vain. I have tried to maintain my dignity and command respect, but it was not easy. All my life people have been jealous of me, and I learned early that I had to be strong to survive. The problems and hurdles I've had to overcome have made me tough. I have learned that life is not equally fair to everyone. Some people are born with more opportunities. Each person simply has to take advantage of those she has.

Because I have not been gushy and gooey, some people have called me haughty. They say I put on airs with my manners and carriage and demeanor, as if I were an aristocrat. Because I'm opinionated and independent and speak my own mind, they may think I'm arrogant and unfeminine. Let me illustrate what I mean. Used to, when we'd have dances, the lady would have a little book that she'd write in the names of young men who wanted to dance with her. Then she danced with the men in the order they signed. One time many years after I'd moved to Louisville, a man said to me, "Mae, you know what we used to do about you at the dances?" I said, "No, what?" He said, "Some of us would get together and say, 'Don't ask Mae for a dance. She's stuck-up. She acts like she's better than we are.'" I said, "What you say may be true, but for some reason I had a partner for every dance."

On the other hand, I know I've had a lot of admirers; some of them I wasn't even aware of. One Sunday a lady friend and I were having dinner down at the Galt House on the river here in Louisville, and as we were leaving my friend went over to speak to a nice-looking couple at another table. While she was talking to the woman, her husband came over to where I was looking out one of the windows at the river and said, "Mrs. Kidd, how are you? May I tell you something?" I said, "Of course." He said, "I have admired and loved you since I've known you. I wish that you had been my wife." That confession surprised and frightened me a little, but all I did was smile and move on. When you've been a public person like me for most of your life, you never know who may be admiring you— or hating you—from a distance. You never know what influence you're having on other people. I think most people have liked me. A lot of people have gone out of their way to tell me the positive impressions they have of me. People have told me they like me because I will fight for what I believe. It is true that I am a fighter, but I fight fairly. I like to make friends, not enemies, even when we disagree. I will, however, raise Cain when I think I or someone else is being treated unfairly. I am a passionate person who can get really riled up.

Believe me when I say I like to bring out the best in people. I try to accentuate the positive when I'm talking about someone. I don't like to tell unpleasant stories. But I know that every life is composed of good things and bad things. I know that if this is to be an accurate account of my life, it has to be balanced—some good and bad, some smiles and cries, some sunshine and rain. I am not ashamed of anything in my life, but there are some things I don't care to tell you about. But maybe I will. I may be as surprised as you to see what will come out. I don't want to disgrace myself, but I have an obligation to tell the truth, the complete truth as I see it and remember it. I must be careful as I talk about certain episodes in my life because I don't want to bring on another stroke. I want to be honest and fair to everyone, myself included. If I misspeak, please understand that it is unintentional.

Unlike a lot of women, I have always loved history. It helps you find out who you are and how you got to be who you are. A history of your life is like a voyage of discovery. I hope that in these reminiscences of my life I can better understand who

With then-governor Wendell Ford

I am. And I hope that my self-discoveries will help you learn
more about yourself too.

I repeat that I'm a sad and helpless old woman, but I know
I can't sit here and rot. Perhaps, as people used to say, I can
redeem the time by telling you about a life that has not been
sad and helpless. Above all, I want to tell you about a life that
is different from anyone else's. I want you to say, as you read
the last page of this book, "There is only one Mae Street Kidd."

Growing Up in Millersburg

To begin at the beginning, I was born Minnie Mae Jones on Main Street in Millersburg and grew up in Shippsville or Shipptown, as it was sometimes called, a small black neighborhood of some fifty families on the outskirts of Millersburg, Kentucky, in the Bluegrass horse country. My mother was a beautiful woman of mixed African, Indian, and white blood. My father was a white farmer from the adjoining Harrison County, just a few miles away. More about them later.

Millersburg was a town of getting along with each other. The people were refined and considerate. Blacks and whites lived close together, and to my knowledge there were never any racial incidents. Everybody was friendly. There was, of course, institutional segregation in the schools and churches. I went to the black school in Millersburg and to a beautiful black Methodist church. Yes indeed, all the people got along with each other, and I'm sure that's why I don't have any bitterness toward whites to this day.

Millersburg was—and still is—a beautiful little aristocratic town. It was planned as the county seat of Bourbon County, but somehow politics got involved and Paris got the courthouse. There's no question but Millersburg is a much prettier town than Paris—and much more cultured. When I was growing up it had two advanced private schools, the Millersburg Military Institute, which is still open, and Millersburg Female College, which is now closed. Kentucky Wesleyan College was founded in Millersburg just before the Civil War and remained there until 1890, when it was moved a few miles away to Winchester. Of course, all that happened before I was born.

In the heart of downtown is the city square with a wrought-iron fence around it. When I was a little girl, every summer we had a chautauqua under a tent on the square. A light opera troupe from Connecticut performed the music of Sigmund Romberg and Gilbert and Sullivan and other composers of light classical music. My mother always bought me a matinee ticket, and she'd take me to the concert and leave me while she went on to work. There were no "white" or "colored" sections, so I sat anywhere I pleased. White women who knew my mother would say with pride, "Why, that's Anna Belle's little girl! How pretty she is all dressed up and ready to listen to good music." As I grew older, I would take myself to the concerts. I never missed one. I was one of the few little girls, white or black, who always attended the chautauqua.

Our little community of Shippsville was about a mile from the downtown. There were a few white farmers that lived a little farther out in the country, but most of the people in our neighborhood were black. Some of the blacks worked for white families, but most of them were farmers who owned or rented their land.

Shippsville didn't have any stores, so everything we bought had to come from Millersburg. When Mother needed anything, she would tell someone in the family to "go in town" to get it. That meant that we had to walk because we didn't have a car or any kind of public transportation. When I got up some size, my parents bought me a pony and a pony cart, which I would drive around the neighborhood and occasionally into town on an errand.

Mother loved beautiful clothes, and she wanted me to be well dressed. She never allowed me to wear worn or torn or dirty dresses. Before school started in the fall, she gave me the privilege of going to the store and buying material for my school dresses, taking it to the seamstress, and telling her how I wanted the dresses made. Easter was a special time for dressing up in

Age six, in Millersburg

our church, and Mother would buy me a new dress and a new hat for Easter Sunday. She let me pick out what I wanted. I have always been especially fond of hats, and to this day I don't think a lady is completely dressed without a hat. As a girl, my hair was very light brown and my mother curled it and tied it with a bow ribbon. One time my new hat had a little streamer on it, and I remember telling the milliner to fix me a little velvet bow to go with it. Believe it or not, but there were three millinery shops in Millersburg, and I could go to any of them and try on hats without embarrassment or restrictions, even though everyone knew I was from a black family. Later, when I got to be a young lady, I often went to Lexington or Paris, where they had larger selections, to buy my dresses and suits. In those towns I never had any problems trying on clothes, though the clerks may have assumed I was white. I never raised the issue, and it never came up.

The "colored" Methodist church that Mae Street Kidd attended as a girl.

A postcard of Millersburg Female College

A postcard of Millersburg Military Institute

The school I went to in Millersburg had four large class-rooms, three teachers, and eight grades with about sixty pupils. There were about twenty in my beginning class, but I don't remember any of them except my stepfather's youngest sister, Everine Taylor. She was a couple of years older than me and relied on me to get her lessons. I had a reputation as a smart kid! We studied everything from cooking or domestic science to geography and math. English was my favorite class because I loved to read, but I also liked history very much.

We were so fortunate to have as principal a lady named Elizabeth Bowen, who had a degree in music and English from Oberlin College in Ohio. She was highly intelligent and talented and even went on to get a master's degree. She was probably the most cultured woman in all of Millersburg, white or black. She was married to the pastor of the Christian church, which my mother belonged to. I just loved her. She taught me piano for two years, but we both soon realized that I didn't have any musical talent. I sang in the church choir, but I wasn't good enough to do solos. I loved poetry, however, and Mrs. Bowen would encourage me to recite poems by Longfellow and Whittier and Bryant in school. I have never forgotten Mrs.

Bowen and her beautiful ways. She is as fresh and beautiful in
my memory as she was when I was a girl.

I was mostly a loner when I was growing up. I was the sort
of child who played by herself a lot. I played mother with my
doll, and I played cooking on my toy stove. I did have an imaginary playmate that I called Helen, who must have been named
after an older neighbor. Sometimes I played with Everine. We
played housekeeping together and made mud pies out in the
yard. We were good friends until she got to be seventeen and
married and moved to Cincinnati. I didn't see much of her
after that. Bourbon County is in Kentucky's horse country, and
I sometimes rode my great-uncle's saddle horse. He was my
mother's uncle and came to live with us from his Harrison
County farm after his wife died. I was never a good horse-
woman because deep down I was afraid of horses! Sometimes
I'd go with my stepfather and mother out to another uncle's
tobacco farm near Millersburg, but I never felt comfortable
out there. I was always afraid of the tobacco worms. I never
played with white children because there were very few out in
Shippsville and because my mother never pushed me among
whites. All in all, I was quite content to be alone and play by
myself.

Most of the real friends I had as a girl were older women.
I have always been attracted to older people. My first husband
was thirteen years older than me. Next to my mother, the
woman I loved most was Mrs. Nellie Henderson, a very handsome woman in her fifties or sixties. On Sunday afternoons
after church I would have dinner at her home on Main Street,
and we would later sit on the swing on her front porch. It may
sound strange, but instead of playing with the other girls, I
preferred to swing with Aunt Nellie and watch the carriages
and cars go by. Just like a grandmother, she would talk to me
about the things girls need to know—church and clothes and
manners. She was lonely, and I guess I was lonely too. We
were two lonely people with a wide age gap who found each
other and became best friends. We loved each other very much.

When I was about thirteen and the flu epidemic hit Millersburg in 1918, she came down with a bad case. I said to my mother, "I want to go over to Aunt Nellie's and take care of her. I don't want her to die." A lot of mothers wouldn't have let their children expose themselves to a disease that was killing thousands and thousands of people, but my mother let me go; and I took care of Aunt Nellie until her son came home from Dayton, Ohio, and took over.

When I was still a girl, Mother got tired of living in the country, so she bought a big eight-room white frame house on Vimont Street in downtown Millersburg. She had a white lawyer cousin named Leer—her maiden name—on her father's side, and he bought the house for her, then transferred the title to her. He bought it because he could ger it cheaper than she could, and there was never any problem with us living in a neighborhood surrounded by white neighbors. The house had three bedrooms upstairs. There was a large double living room with sliding doors between them. Right after my stepfather died, Mother took the big dining room and made it into a bedroom for herself downstairs. The house was on a corner lot with huge trees on either side, and at nighttime in summer I had to sleep with a sheet over me because of the coolness from the trees.

I think I was fortunate to grow up in Millersburg. It may have been a solitary life, but I think it was a happy one that provided me a good foundation for my later careers in business and politics. More important than the place itself, however, I was lucky to grow up in a good family—though it was by no means a traditional one, as you will see.

First, let me tell you about my mother, Anna Belle Leer Taylor. Picture her: a beautiful woman of mixed blood, with gorgeous hair like silk. When people told me I looked like her, I was flattered. She lived to a great age and died in 1984 at 101 in a nursing home in Mt. Sterling. Almost all her life was spent in Millersburg, and she loved living there. When she got very old and feeble, I asked if she wanted to move to Louisville to

be with me. She said no. She wanted to live out her life close
to where she was born and had lived her beautiful life. Mother
loved flowers and shrubs and had one of the most gorgeous
yards in town. She especially liked roses and tulips and had
lovely potted plants like ferns and geraniums and begonias. I
got my love for flowers and a pretty yard from her.

Unlike many women of color in Millersburg, she never
worked as a domestic for white families. Sometimes she would
cook meals for them in an emergency; then she went into the
catering business and made a marvelous reputation for her
delicious food. She was famous for her cakes and pies. People
would bring their food for her to prepare for special occasions—
a wedding or a big family reunion or a party—and then pick it
up. Sometimes she would serve the food and would hire young
black people to assist her. She would never, ever allow me to
wait on white people! She catered for many of the richest white
families in Central Kentucky. Earlier she had trained with one
of the local white doctors to be a midwife, and she delivered
dozens of babies, sometimes with the doctor and sometimes
alone. One time she went with one of her pregnant patients
to New York just in case the baby arrived before the woman
returned home.

She was very, very strict with me. I couldn't do anything
without asking her. One time I told her I was leaving to catch
the bus to go to Lexington to shop. She said, "Well, you didn't
tell me anything about it." I was eighteen and was already supporting myself selling insurance, but I said, "May I go?" She
said, "No, you may not. You didn't discuss it with me, so you're
not going." I didn't go. There was no appeal. There was nothing I could do, unless, of course, I had chosen to disobey my
mother. And I would never have done that. No, her action
didn't surprise me at all. I had forgotten to consult her, and
she was punishing me. It had happened before, and it would
happen again. When she did give me permission to go on trips
away from home, I had to tell her where I was going, who I

Mother, Anna Belle Leer Taylor

would see, where I would be staying, what I would be doing, and when I would be back home.

It did not even upset me when she told me I couldn't go. I had been used to her strictness all my life. I remember once when we had a big summer camp meeting at our church in Millersburg. There was a tent pitched on a lot next to the church house, and people had little booths where they could sell fish and chicken and pies and cakes to make money. Guest evangelists preached every afternoon and evening. A nice young man—as fair as I am—was standing with me outside the tent, and we were talking before going inside for the afternoon service. He was born in Millersburg but had moved to Detroit and had known my mother and family all his life. Mother saw me talking with him, walked over, and without a word of warning, slapped my face, and said, "Get inside that tent!" What did I do? I went inside the tent. I was stunned but I had always obeyed my mother. I know she could have called me over and told me quietly not to talk with the boy. Instead, she slapped me in public without warning. Although she had known the boy since he was born, he was now a city boy, and she didn't trust him with me. I was a pretty girl, and he was a good-looking boy. She didn't want me to have anything to do with him. She was fiercely protective of me. Maybe she thought he would try to lure me to Detroit. I don't really know what she thought because we never mentioned the incident again. She never offered an explanation, and I never asked her for one. That was the way she was. As long as I lived under her roof, I had to obey her rules. I was used to her ways.

She never told me about sex. She just said, "Stay away from men and boys—at least until you're married." That was it. Like most children, what little I knew about sex I learned from older children at school. At recess, when the older girls would huddle together to talk about boys, I would slip up and listen to them. My mother never allowed me to have a boyfriend as long as I lived at home. If I wanted a social life of any kind, it had to be in a group. When I got older, the young people from our church might gather on Sunday afternoons at someone's house to sing religious songs and eat ice cream that we made in a hand-turned freezer. We always stayed as a group. We never paired off. Of course, some of my classmates had boyfriends and girlfriends when they were fifteen or sixteen years old, but I didn't. Boys were off limits to me until I left home and moved to Louisville. In fact, when that time came Mother bought me a new trunk, and my stepfather gave me money for new clothes; they both went to the train station to see me off. Then I was on my own and could run my own life and make my own decisions.

Everybody in Millersburg liked and respected my mother. She was called "the mayor of Millersburg." People liked her plain-spoken manner. They liked the way she raised us children. In those days people owned their children. Of course, I can now see that she had her dark side. She lacked warmth. She was sharp and unrelenting. She was often cold and aloof. I know that I inherited some of those qualities from her, and I have tried to soften and overcome them. I wanted to be warmer and friendlier than she was. I have tried to soften the edges as much as I could, but I know deep down that I will always be my mother's daughter. I know that, for better or worse, I carry her genes and her personality traits.

Indeed, from my mother I learned to be proud of who I was. Even while she was being a hard taskmaster, she was teaching me lessons in life. I was required to help with the housework, and I was required to work on my lessons until they were done. I knew that in her closet was my stepfather's razor strap with my mother behind it. Many of our black neighbors did cleaning and washing and ironing for white families, but Mother would never allow me to work for other people. She would absolutely forbid me to work for white families, even as a babysitter. She said, "Mae, I have to serve other people because I don't have a choice. I want you to have a choice when you grow up. As long as I am able, I will not let you be a servant for white people." Thus I grew up with a good self-image. By her deeds, Mother taught me that I was as good as anybody. I never developed a servant mentality. She trained me to do household chores at home so I could do them when I had a home of my own, but she never allowed me to do them for anybody else, white or black.

When my mother was about twenty-four years old, she married a black man named James William Taylor. I was two years old and my brother George William was four. He was the finest stepfather I could hope for. Everyone called him Willie but me. I called him Wowley, the name I called him when I was a baby. He called me Sister and was very fond of me. I think he called me Sister because that's what he wanted his own children to call me. He considered me his own daughter, but he never tried to boss me. He was gentle with all of us. Sometimes he would speak sternly to us, but he never whipped us. He left that up to Mother. Of course, she would have done that anyway. He let mother raise me her way and never interfered when she was reprimanding me. He was a wonderful man, always a gentleman. He was easy to get along with and did whatever Mother wanted to do. I never heard them argue or fight. He was a man of few words. He sometimes liked a little bourbon, but I never saw him drunk or violent. He was a trustee of the CME Church and became a thirty-second degree Mason.

He and my mother worked hard to provide for our family. He and another man leased some land and had a ten-acre tobacco base. Tobacco was his cash crop, and that's what we lived on. When he got older, he stopped his tobacco farming and started a chicken business. He raised them in large brooders where their feet never touched the ground. When they got big enough to eat, he and Mother would kill and dress the chickens for customers. People would call in their orders for so many chickens, and when they arrived, the chickens would be dressed and ready to go.

We were a family that provided for ourselves, and we raised most of what we ate. Mother was an industrious woman and a wonderful homemaker. We had chickens for eating and for eggs. We raised our own hogs and killed them when it got cold and we could keep the meat from spoiling by salting it down or smoking it. We ate vegetables out of our garden for half a year, and in the winter we ate what Mother had canned and preserved. About the only foods we bought at the grocery store were flour, sugar, coffee, and salt. Mother was also a very good quilter. In the wintertime I used to help her piece quilt tops by the fireplace. Then we put up the quilting frame and with the help of her mother-in-law, we made each top into a quilt by sewing them to a backing with a cotton batting in between. I still have some of her beautiful quilts, and they are treasures. Since I've become almost blind, I'm afraid people will steal from me; so when my sister was here the last time, I told her to take my favorite one, called the Double Wedding Ring.

My mother and my stepfather's mother were very good friends. They lived close to our house in Shippsville, and we did a lot of things together—quilting and preserving and cooking. Mrs. Taylor lived in an old frame house with lots of land around it. We were a family-oriented people and often ate dinner and supper with each other. We didn't entertain friends very much but were always having family gatherings, especially at Thanksgiving and Christmas. My stepfather and my mother owned jointly the house we lived in. She had her own income but shared it with him when he was short.

I was already in school when my half brother, Webster Demetrius Taylor, and half sister, Mary Evelyn Taylor, came along. I think they were a surprise to Mother because she was forty-two when Demetrius was born and forty-three when Mary Evelyn was born. As I have said, we all considered ourselves one family, even though my brother George and I carried our father's name of Jones. It was not unusual in those days for the children of a white father and a colored mother to take the father's name and be acknowledged in the community. Of course, we were not taken into our father's home and raised as his legitimate children, but everyone knew who we were.

Now I'm getting into a murky area that I don't know much about. People did not talk about matters of sex and children of mixed relationships. My mother never, ever mentioned my father. Of course, when I got up some size I was curious about my real father, but I never asked her about it. It wasn't considered any of my business. I do know, however, that my mother was born on a farm in Harrison County, which adjoined Bourbon County. It may have been a farm owned by my father's family, and she may have worked in the house as a cook or maid. Now I'm speculating because I don't know anything for sure, but she and my father may have gotten to know each other because they both were growing up on the same farm—she as a black servant girl and he as the rich white farmer's son. Look at the situation. She was a very pretty girl, almost white. He was a good-looking young white boy. White men liked to seduce pretty colored girls. That's why we had so many beautiful, light-skinned Negro children in Millersburg. Maybe one day she noticed him and he noticed her. You can guess what happened. A young colored servant girl did whatever the white boss, or the white boss's son, said. Maybe as time went on they fell in love. I believe they did because they had two children, and their relationship must have continued for a number of years—else my mother would have married before she did. They both knew from the beginning that he *couldn't* marry her. She surely knew that even if he could, he *wouldn't* marry her. After all, he was from a rich, land-owning family, and it would have destroyed his future. Mixed-race marriages were not possible, according to the law or the custom. The custom was that white men seduced young women of color, and sometimes the two young people were deeply in love. Sometimes their relationships continued for a long time, sometimes throughout their lives. It was very common. When you're young and in love, you don't worry about society's prejudices and laws. Who knows? Their relationship may have continued for a long, long time—maybe after he married a white woman and after she married a black man. We do know that it lasted long enough for two children—my brother George and me—to be born.

Nobody in my family ever mentioned my father to me. The situation that my family and I were in was considered just as natural as the trees around our house. They were just there, and I never asked who planted them or where they came from. What little knowledge I had of my father and his family came from older women of color. I'd be at somebody's house and we'd be talking—a little girl and an older woman—and she'd say, "Mae, I do declare you're just like your grandmother Elizabeth Jones. You look like her. You act like her. You even put powder and rouge on your face like her." I grew up knowing not to ask my mother or my stepfather about my real father. Nothing was ever said by either one of them about it. Indeed, I don't think it bothered Mr. Taylor that my mother had two children by a white man before he married her. It was not that uncommon. And what could he have done anyway?

I'm hesitant to talk about my blood father because light people of color like me are sometimes accused of bragging about their white blood. I had nothing to do with my racial makeup. I didn't choose my mother or my father. I know almost nothing about my father, except that he was a white farmer from Harrison County, Kentucky, and his name was Charles Robert Jones. That much is on my birth certificate. I do know that he eventually married a white woman and had another set of children by her, and they and their mother used to come visit my mother, who was very friendly with his white family. But I never wanted anything to do with them. I was hurt that he couldn't—or wouldn't—acknowledge me openly as his daughter. It was a painful part of my childhood, but I got over it.

I only saw my father one time. It was after I was grown and living in Louisville. I was visiting my mother in Millersburg and was in the post office when he came in. A friend who was with me said, "Mae, see that white man over there at the counter? That's your father." I looked over at him but didn't say anything. He made no move to speak to me, and I didn't speak to him. He left the post office and then came back in almost immediately. Again, he looked over in my direction but didn't say anything. He stood without moving for a minute or two, then left again. I believe he recognized me and came back in to take a second look at his daughter. No, I wasn't resentful that my own father didn't speak to me. At that point in my life,

I didn't give a damn! It was too late to make a difference to
me. I remember that everyone in my father's family was crazy
about my brother George. They provided some support for
him and recognized him as a member of the family among
themselves. It is possible, of course, that my father gave my
mother some money for my support, but if he did, she never
told me. All I know is that my father never made an effort to
get to know me, and I never tried to get to know him. I was
never interested in becoming friendly with any of my father's
people. I didn't care anything about them. I didn't hate them.
I had no feelings about them at all. For me, they simply
didn't—and don't—exist.

My brother was much fairer than I am. He was a beautiful man. He was reared by the same great aunt out in the country that raised my mother. He would ride his horse into town
to attend the black school. He put his horse up at the livery
stable just like the white boys, and when school was out, he
would ride his horse back to our aunt's farm. He was white
enough that he could have gone to the white school, but everyone knew who his mother was. My mother wanted us to be
close as brother and sister, so she sent me to live in the country with him and my aunt and uncle for two weeks each summer. Sometimes he'd put me on his horse behind him and
make it trot and I would be scared to death. I'd hold on for
dear life. He called our great aunt Mama and he called our
mother Mother. He married a black woman and became fore-
man of a coal and lumber company. When he passed in 1987,
all our white relatives attended his funeral.

I never had any contact with my father's family. When my
white half sisters visited my mother in Millersburg, I was never
there. I just heard about it. When I was a student at Lincoln
Institute and would go home for Christmas, my brother might
say, "Oh, your sisters came over to see us." But we never talked
about them being there. I have been told that one of my white
half sisters is still living. That's all I know about them. That's
all I care to know about them.

On the other hand, I was quite close to my black brothers and sisters and had good relations with them through the years. They were all successful and lived good lives—due largely I think to my mother's good influence. She was always pushing and encouraging us to improve ourselves. But in many ways, I was the pivot of the family. After my stepfather passed, my mother continued to live in her big house in Millersburg, but she told me she wanted either a gun or a dog. My stepfather had been a hunter, but my mother could not have shot a gun if her life had depended upon it. So I decided a dog would be better for her, even though I've never cared much for pets. One day I saw a collie advertised in the Louisville paper, and a friend and I drove out to inspect the dog. He was so beautiful, with a white band around his neck and white legs. I bought him and took him to Mother. Soon he was able to open the screen door, and at nighttime he slept at the foot of her bed with his feet sprawled out. Mother loved him. It wasn't that she was afraid to stay by herself. She was simply lonely and wanted the dog for company.

Finally, Mother got too old and feeble to live by herself, so she sold her house to a white preacher and moved to Paris, Kentucky, and lived in a house next door to my sister and her husband. Then when she was about ninety-eight years old she became very ill, and a young white doctor who had been her paperboy in Millersburg said to my sister, "I'm going to put your mother in a good nursing home. She can't live by herself any longer." He said he loved my mother dearly, and she loved him. Each day when he delivered her paper, she had a piece of cake or pie saved for him. He was a young man, but he already had a terminal cancer and didn't have long to live. He said he wanted to get my mother placed in a nursing home before he died. And he did. She went into a nursing home in Mt. Sterling and lived there about three years before she died at the age of 101. Indeed, almost all my immediate family is dead now. Mother passed in 1984, brother George William in 1986, and brother Webster Demetrius in 1988. My sister Mary

Evelyn, who lives in Paris, Kentucky, is the only surviving member of our family.

Yes, I had a beautiful family, and it was a well educated one for that time. The black school in Millersburg didn't go beyond the eighth grade, so my mother sent me to the Lincoln Institute, a boarding school for blacks from all over Kentucky at Simpsonville, out in the country near Shelbyville. It was founded by Berea College after the Day Law prohibited the teaching of blacks and whites together in any kind of school, public or private. Until 1904, blacks and whites in Berea had been taught in the same classrooms. The institute was really a kind of prep school and teachers college. People from Lincoln went all over the state to recruit children to come to Lincoln and complete high school. I left home and enrolled at Lincoln in 1919, when I was fifteen years old. When I arrived there I found a beautiful campus and farm and young black people from counties that didn't have enough blacks to support a high school. The institute offered many vocational programs as well as a course in teacher training.

I lived on campus in one of the dormitories and studied a course in home economics. It's been so long ago I don't remember many of my classmates or teachers, but I do remember that Lincoln was a place of love and harmony and hard work. Although the students were all black, we had an integrated faculty, and many of our teachers were from the North. I did have a little boyfriend who carried my books around campus from class to class. I wasn't serious about him. In fact, I didn't have a kissing boyfriend during my teenage years. We couldn't have gone out on dates, even if we had wanted to. The rules of the school didn't allow dating. We had socials like picnics and sports activities where boys and girls could mingle and work off a lot of energy, but there was no pairing off. I don't believe that dances were permitted on campus. It was a very strict school, and we were expected to be on our best behavior all the time.

I had completely forgotten my little boyfriend's name until

I read his obituary a few days ago. His name was Charles Edward Powell, and the write-up said he lived on the Allendale Farm in Shelby County and worked at the Kentucky Children's Home. He was married and had several children. I remember him as a lovely person, but his wife was welcome to him. I don't think we would have had a good life together.

In addition to our classes and sports, we had to work to help pay for our expenses. The institute was located on several hundred acres of land, and a lot of it was cultivated by the students to grow food for the lunchroom. In home economics classes, I helped can food from the gardens that we would eat during the winter months. At that time I had a nice little voice, and I helped to promote the institute in churches and schools as a member of the Lincoln Quartet.

Lincoln was a wonderful experience for me, and I have happy memories of my two years there. I wish that I had been able to finish school at Lincoln and maybe become a teacher, but because of family financial problems, I had to drop out during my junior year when I was seventeen. It didn't cost much to send me to Lincoln, but my family just couldn't afford even that small amount. I was downcast at having to leave, but I never held a grudge against my mother or stepfather. They did as much for me as they could.

During my time at Lincoln the president was the Rev. A. Eugene Thomas, but the president I knew best was Whitney M. Young, Sr., who served from the mid-thirties until the school closed in 1966. Whitney appointed me a school trustee after World War II, and I served for more than ten years. When I was student at Lincoln, I would sometimes help prepare food for the trustees at Mr. Thomas's home. We would set the tables with beautiful china and nice linens, and someone would serve as the lookout and say, "Here comes the board. Here comes the board." That would be the signal to get to our work stations so that we could serve dinner to the board. Little did I dream then that someday I would be a member of that board.

Now that black and white children go to school together,

there's no need for Lincoln Institute. After it closed in 1966, it became a Job Corps Center for a while. Then the state transferred the property to the Lincoln Foundation, and for several more years it was a center for educating exceptional children. I was in the General Assembly when the vote was taken to close it. I fought hard to keep it open, but the representative from Shelbyville led the drive to close it, and he won. I remember so well the night the vote was taken. The school faculty were in the balcony hoping and praying it would stay open, and I was down on the legislative floor fighting hard, with tears running down my cheeks. But they closed it anyway. It's still a sacred spot for me as well as many other blacks who went to school there. We probably got a better education at Lincoln than we would have gotten if we could have attended the whites-only schools in our home counties.

Remember that my mother would never hire me out to anybody when I was a young girl, but I was 17 when I left Lincoln and I had to do something to earn money. I was lucky enough to become an agent for Mammoth Life and Accident Insurance Company, a black-owned and operated company based in Louisville. Mother heard that the agent who worked our part of the state was going to retire, so she asked the company supervisor if I could have his job. He said, "How old is she?" Mother said, "She's seventeen but very mature for her age." After he interviewed me, he said, "All right, we'll give her a try." I really wasn't old enough and didn't have any experience in the insurance business, but he must have been impressed with me.

My territory included Millersburg, and Carlisle, another little nearby town in Nicholas County, and my job was to sell policies and collect what we called industrial premiums, which were about 35 or 50 cents a week. They were sickness and accident policies that paid small benefits if a person got sick or had an accident. We also had burial policies that could pay as much as $850 for funeral expenses. Later on, the company began offering ordinary or life insurance, which paid amounts like $10,000 to your heirs at your death. The company soon found out that I was a good salesman and a good representative.

Every two weeks I had to catch the bus and go to Carlisle to collect premiums and sell new policies. The premiums were so low it wasn't worth my time to collect them every week. My mother was a little anxious about me having to ride on the bus by myself, but it was something I had to do. From the bus station it might be half a mile or more to the black neighborhoods where I had customers. I had to walk everywhere I went, but I was young and strong, and it didn't bother me at all. I was never scared because I was carrying money and collecting money for premiums. Nobody ever robbed or even threatened me. I never had any bad experiences anywhere because everybody knew my parents in Millersburg, and in Carlisle I soon became known and the older people began watching over me. Some days I'd collect close to a hundred dollars, and that was a lot of money in those days. I knew a black doctor and his wife in Carlisle, and they invited me to spend the noon hour with them. I'd pack my lunch and eat it with them and rest before I resumed my work in the afternoon. After a long day of walking from house to house in the black neighborhoods, I'd catch the bus back to Millersburg.

As a salesman, I had to develop my own techniques of salesmanship. I'd never taken a business course in school, so I had to rely on my instincts and common sense. I soon discovered that my best source of new customers was the friends of my friends. Another good source was newcomers who moved into the community. I started out knocking on doors, then after I moved to Louisville and had access to telephones, I called to make an appointment. That is, I called people who had telephones. Back then, most black people didn't have telephones, regardless of where they lived. Whether I was talking at the door or on the phone, I would say something like, "Hello, I'm Mae Jones. I'm a representative of Mammoth Life and Accident Insurance Company, and I'd like to talk with you about some valuable services we can provide for you and your family." After I was invited to the prospect's home, we would sit down and I would get out my salesman's book and start asking questions about the family—how many children, the ages of parents and children, where they worked—questions like that. I had to find out family and financial information so I could tailor a policy to their needs and ability to pay. People who made only a few dollars a week couldn't afford high-premium life insurance.

Everybody in Millersburg was proud of my success because I was only a teenager but I conducted myself like a grown woman. At seventeen I opened my own bank account. I kept my business records and sent reports and the premium money to the home office in Louisville every two weeks. For a young black girl, I was making good money. I didn't get a straight salary but was paid a commission of 20 percent of the premium money I sent in. My insurance work only took about two days out of every two weeks, so I had plenty of time to busy myself with church activities and to be active in the children's auxiliary of the Masonic Lodge. My stepfather was active in the Masons, and my mother was a member of the Eastern Star Auxiliary. Mother didn't push me into community work, but she expected me to be busy and productive all the time. That's a pattern that has stayed with me all my life. It's one of the many debts I owe my mother. Indeed, with her strict, no-nonsense manner and her own version of tough love, she had prepared me for the most important move in my life. She taught me how to survive on my own as a single black woman with a limited education.

Surviving and Thriving
in Louisville

I had been working as an agent for Mammoth Life and Accident Insurance Company for about four years when there was a bad tornado in Lexington. People came from everywhere to see the damage. Mr. W.H. Wright came with his adopted daughter, Lucille Fitzpatrick, who had been a friend of mine since I met her at an annual meeting of company agents in Louisville. Mr. Wright was president of Mutual Savings Bank, a black bank in Louisville, and was chairman of the Mammoth Board of Trustees. He had come to Lexington to check on the damages and to see how much money Mammoth would have to pay out. I was talking with them when he suddenly said, "Mae, I've heard about the good work you're doing for the company as an agent. Would you be interested in working for the company in Louisville?" I said I would, and he said I'd hear from him soon.

In about two weeks I had a letter from Mr. H.E. Hall, the president of Mammoth, saying that Mr. Wright had recommended me for a job and inviting me to move to Louisville. You can imagine how excited I was! I talked it over with my parents, and they agreed that it was a good opportunity for me. My mother bought me a new trunk to put my clothes in and came down to the train station to see me off. We both shed tears, of course, because we knew that I was leaving home for good. Except for the time I spent at Lincoln Institute, it would be the first time I'd ever lived away from home. I knew I would miss my mother, but I also knew that sooner or later I would have to leave. I was about twenty-one years old, and I knew the time had come.

I made arrangements to move in with my friend Lucille, who lived on Magazine Street with her mother. I lived with them as a member of the family and ate my breakfast and supper at their house. I ate my lunch at work at the company cafeteria. Lucille also worked at Mammoth and we saw a good deal of each other. I was fortunate that she helped to introduce me to Louisville. I knew that she was at least partly responsible for me getting my job. After an apartment opened up in the Mammoth Building, Lucille and I moved there. The company used to have twenty-four apartments to rent, but as their business grew, they took over more and more space until all the apartments were eliminated. Lucille and I lived together smoothly until we got a third roommate. I felt crowded and moved out. That's when I moved to the street I'm still living on, Chestnut Street. For about two years I lived with Dr. and Mrs. Robert Oliver just one block from this house; then I moved to another address on Chestnut. Finally, I moved into this very house and rented an upstairs bedroom from a widow named Mahin until I married my first husband. I lived with families because in those days it wasn't considered proper for young single women to live in apartments. It was all right for Lucille and me to live in an apartment at the Mammoth Building because that's where we worked. But that was an exception to the rule.

My mother had told me that one of the first things I should do when I got to Louisville was to join the church. "The best people," she said, "are in church, and I want you to know the best people in Louisville." The second Sunday I was in town, therefore, I moved my church membership to the C.M.E. Church, a Methodist church. I also became active in the YWCA and made a place for myself in it. We had sorority and fraternity dances at the "colored" YMCA at Tenth and Chestnut in the ballroom on the tenth floor. It was a beautiful place with large windows. At the dances each young lady was given a little book in which young men wrote their names if you agreed to dance with them. A man would walk up and say, "May I see your book?" He'd look at it and say, "You've already got one, two, three, and four reserved. May I have the fifth dance with you?" If you wanted to dance with him, you'd say yes, and he would write his name on that line. When the fifth dance started, he'd walk over to you and claim his dance. I was always escorted to the dances by a friend, but I was free to dance with anyone I wanted.

It wasn't until the 1960s that Louisville became a truly integrated city where blacks could go anyplace they pleased. We had a few little eating places and places to socialize, but most of the entertaining was done in homes. Years later, after I was married, my husband and I would go to dinner in the homes of friends and business associates. We entertained each other with bridge parties, especially in the early forties, when bridge was so popular. I also belonged to a women's bridge club that met once a month, but I finally had to quit it because it was taking up too much of my time. After World War II, when I had established myself as a businesswoman, I organized the Business and Professional Club for black women and was active in it for many years. Because of the way I walked and dressed, clubs were always calling on me to organize style shows. You see, when I first arrived in Louisville, I attracted a lot of attention because of the way I looked—my color, my stature, my poise, the way I walked and talked and conducted myself. When I walked past, I could hear people say, "Who's that beautiful woman? She must be new to town."

There were very few first-rate places for blacks to stay and eat. All the hotels, restaurants, and cafeterias on Fourth Street were off limits to us. I never tried to go into any of those fancy downtown cafes, though I would have been able to pass for white if I'd wanted to. I never tried. I never wanted to put myself into what could have been an embarrassing situation. But I am an American citizen. I have always been an American citizen. That gives me certain rights, regardless of customs and

As a young woman in Louisville

laws. If I went into a clothing store and wanted to try on a dress or a hat, then I had the right to do it. The sales clerks had something to sell and I wanted to buy it; therefore, it was never a matter of whether or not I was "passing" for white—or for any other color. I would have been simply expressing myself as a free American. But the issue never came up in Louisville. I never had to say what I was thinking: I may be classified as a Negro, a second-class citizen, but I'm first of all an American citizen; and I have the right to shop here and try on and buy what you have to sell. But no clerk ever said to me, "Oh, I'm sorry, but we think you're black, and we can't serve you." I will repeat it: I never made an issue of my race. I let people think or believe what they wanted to. If it was ever a problem, then it was their problem, not mine. I never, ever advertised my race, and I still don't. The Declaration of Independence says we're all created equal, and I believe it.

I can honestly say I never saw a black person in Louisville embarrassed in public by being denied any service or admission. I'm sure it happened, but I was not present. Of course, Louisville was a Southern city and we had some Jim Crow laws, but most of us blacks knew what the boundaries were and more or less observed them. What were those boundaries? I couldn't use the main public library. I couldn't go to the first-run movie shows on Fourth Street. I had to attend the "colored" theaters like the Lyric and the Grand. I couldn't stay or eat in the Brown Hotel. As long as we kept within those boundaries, we never had any problems. The time came in the forties and fifties when blacks and whites began to test those boundaries. We did it in many different ways. I had my own methods that suited who I was, and I will tell you more about them later.

When I arrived in Louisville as a single black woman, my first concern was survival. That meant that I had to spend most of my time and energy doing my work and pleasing my employers. My first job at Mammoth was working as a file clerk with policy lapses. It was mainly a clerical position. I sat on a high stool like the one I'm sitting on now in this kitchen and worked out of a large file cabinet. I'd check the policies that had lapsed so that we could try to get the holders to reinstate them. My next job was assistant bookkeeper in the office where we kept track of money coming in and going out. I was good in math and had studied bookkeeping in high school. It was a slight promotion over my first job and paid a little more money than the $21 a week I made at first. I knew if I did my job right, I'd get small raises every few months. I spent almost all I

made on my food and lodging and clothing. But I started doing something that may surprise you. On my second payday, I
started sending my mother $5 each week. She didn't ask for it
and didn't really expect it, but it was something I wanted to do
to show her how much I loved and missed her. Indeed, every
Sunday for a long time I got lonesome for her and cried.

I didn't have enough money to go home very often, but
when I did I tried to carry Mother a little present—maybe a
scarf or a small bottle of perfume. There was good train service between Louisville and Millersburg, but I usually took
the bus because it was cheaper. Incidentally, whenever I was
traveling around Kentucky, I always sat where I wanted to and
nobody ever questioned me. Of course, if I had been darker, I
might have been required to sit in the "colored" sections. I
never told anybody I had black blood and nobody ever asked.

After I'd been in my new job for a few months, the head
of the department came to me and said, "You're now our assistant bookkeeper, and our head bookkeeper is leaving. Would
you like to have his job?" I said, "No, I don't believe I would."
He said, "Why not?" I said, "Once a bookkeeper, always a bookkeeper. I don't want a dead-end job. I don't want to be a bookkeeper all my life. I'll just keep the job I have until something
I want comes along. I don't care if it pays a little more money."
Sure enough, before long I was offered a job in the policy issue office. Finally, after the company officers saw what a good
job I was doing, I was made supervisor of policy issue and held
the job for about nine years. Every policy application came
through me. I had to approve every one to make sure it was a
good risk for us. By the time I left Mammoth to go work with
the Red Cross in England during World War II, I had made a
good track record for myself with the company.

I was away from Mammoth for a couple of years with the
Red Cross and then with United Seamen's Service in Portland, Maine, and returned to Louisville in 1946. During the
war if you were involved in the war effort, you were supposed
to get your old job back when you came home. That was the

A promotion for Mammoth Insurance featuring
Count Basie

law. My former secretary was given my job as supervisor of
policy issue while I was away, and she was so afraid that I wanted
that job back she would hardly speak to me. Well, I didn't want
my old job at all. I had something else in mind.

While I was away, I became familiar with a new dimension of public service and business called public relations, and
I wanted to develop a program for Mammoth. At that time,
not many companies knew anything about public relations—
certainly nobody at Mammoth. During my Red Cross work I
had learned of the importance of public relations in creating
good will between officers and enlisted men and between the

At the annual Mammoth picnic

military and the public. In Portland I had held a position that
was almost completely in the field of public relations. I was
convinced that I could put to good use what I had learned for
Mammoth. I spent three months reading books and articles
and designing a proposal for a public relations program and
then made my presentation before the board of directors. I
convinced the board that it would be a great asset to the company, and I was made director of the program with a desk in
the front office with my own secretary and two other staff members. For a year I traveled to our twenty-eight branch offices in
the eight states where we did business — Kentucky, Tennessee,
Indiana, Michigan, Wisconsin, Illinois, Ohio, and Missouri —
and explained the new program and how to implement it.

   Overall, the program was designed to present Mammoth
as a service-oriented company whose main concern was the
welfare of the policyholder. One of our first goals was to improve communications between our clients and ourselves. Prior
to my work, each branch office wrote its own advertising and

Presenting scholarship checks from Mammoth at a
commencement ceremony at Lincoln Institute

public announcements, and most of it was poorly done. It was
often unclear and sometimes even ungrammatical. The new
program required that all branch communications had to be
approved by the central office. With a central office of communications we could maintain quality control. All letters to
policyholders had to come from the Louisville office, which I
headed for eighteen years.

My work concentrated on internal company communications, on public relations and press conferences, and on various kinds of company-sponsored meetings. One of my
innovations was a big banquet each year to recognize outstanding agents. At our first dinner in Madison, Wisconsin, we had
a big press conference with all the big wheels in the insur-

In her office at Mammoth with a student partici-
pating in the Executive for a Day program

ance business present. We had a lovely dinner, then the awards,
and finally an elegant dance. It was the sort of occasion that
created good will for the company with its employees and with
the public.

I also started a twenty-five-year club, which employees were
inducted into after they had put in the required years of service. Every year we held a banquet in a different city to honor
those people and gave them a beautiful pin and an award. Our
meetings and dinners were all big successes because we organized them professionally and spent enough money to make
them first class.

There were so many facets to our program that I can't recall them all. I started a promotion called Executive for a Day,
when we would select young black people from local schools
and have them substitute for the company executives. One
Christmas I heard of a little girl with a terminal illness who
wanted an electric train, and I saw to it that Mammoth got
one for her. It made a lot of good will for the company and
was written up in the *Louisville Defender* and the *Courier-Journal*. I took advantage of every opportunity to publicize the com-

The *Belle of Louisville* before a cruise for Mammoth employees

On the *Belle of Louisville*

At a meeting for Mammoth agents and managers in Chicago

pany and put it in a favorable light. I tried to push forward the
company president and the other executives, but sometimes
the newspapers insisted that my picture be put in the paper.
"You're the best-looking representative Mammoth has," they
said.

    But my work wasn't easy. I had to jump obstacles and over-
come prejudice against women. Even after I wrote my public
relations proposal and the board approved it, a man on the
board said he wanted to be its director. I had come back to
Louisville with a plan that I thought would help make Mammoth into a big company. I had the idea, and I did all the
work. But a man got the position that should have been mine.
What could I do? That's the way men treated women in those
days. A man got the title and the pay, and my staff and I did all
the work.

    In 1957, when I began to organize a credit union at the
company, several men tried to stop me. One of the female officers of the company tried to keep me from having meetings.

At a meeting for Mammoth agents and managers in Cincinnati

But I went right on because I knew it was something the employees needed and would support. It was a sort of bank in which employees deposited so much money each payday, and then they could borrow from it when they needed to. They would also earn interest on the money they deposited. It's like a savings and loan association, except it's restricted to the employees of a single company. Our credit union had its own officers and two full-time employees, and we had hundreds of members because it covered employees from all the districts in which we did business. The credit union became a big business, and I organized it.

The National Negro Insurance Association heard about my work at Mammoth and asked me to organize a public relations program for them. I didn't get much of a salary from the association, but I had all my travel expenses paid to meetings all over the country. In 1948 I organized a public relations program for the seventy-two black insurance companies that comprised the NNIA.

One of my major achievements as PR director for the as-

sociation was a rail tour I organized to the convention in Los
Angeles. We occupied eight sleeping cars, a VistaDome and a
diner. I was beginning to make a national name for myself. I
was even accepted as a member of the American Public Relations Association. In fact, my husband Mr. Street and I were
just about the only people at Mammoth who ever started anything new. He was responsible for the department that took
care of sick and death claims. No one else at the company
had enough imagination and sense to do the things we did.
Yet when I tried to help the company with my innovations,
they did their best to keep me down. Well, I showed them! My
attitude was this: "All right, I won't fuss with you, but just try
to keep me down. If you knock me down, I'll not only get up
but I'll rise higher than I was before." One time I wrote an
article for our PR quarterly about the cork the fish keeps pulling down under the water, but it keeps popping up. That's the
way I was.

People kept trying to pull me down under the water and
drown me, but I kept popping up. Let me give you an example.
I took a year's leave of absence one time to work with a cosmetics firm in Detroit, and when I came home I expected to
get my old job back in public relations. Instead, they had given
my job permanently to the daughter of one of the founders.
That woman didn't know what to do with the job. She didn't
even want the job. She just wanted the title and the salary. I
pleaded with the president to give me back my old job. I reminded him that I had created the department, made it a big
success, and had put Mammoth on the map. But he said, "No,
you must take the examination and sell ordinary insurance."
That was a dirty deal! I had done so much for him and the
company. I had placed many articles about him in the paper
and helped to make him a big man. I was very angry and determined to turn the tables on him. He wanted to embarrass
me by sending me back to selling ordinary insurance, but I
embarrassed him by selling more insurance than anyone in
the history of the company. Nobody had ever sold a quarter of

a million dollars worth of insurance at Mammoth. I did! Nobody embarrasses Mae Street Kidd—not in the long run! I've got too many guts in me to let you embarrass me. I will do the dirty job you give me better than anybody ever did it—and better than you ever dreamed I could.

After I set the company record for insurance sales, I was asked to take my old job back, and I agreed to. Why not? After all, it was my job. I created it and I knew how the job should be done. So I went back and resumed doing projects and programs that had been so successful before—the public relations releases, the twenty-five-year club, the internal communications. People were glad to see me back in my old position. Of the more than forty years I worked at Mammoth, I spent some eighteen years in public relations. It was my favorite job because I had made it from nothing.

But that honeymoon didn't last long. I began to feel hemmed in by the company, restless and unfulfilled, and not respected for the work I was doing. So one year I obtained a leave of absence and worked in Chicago and Detroit for Fuller Products, a cosmetics company. I got the job through a friend who lived in Chicago and worked for the company. One day she took me by the office and introduced me to Mr. Fuller, a self-made millionaire. Before I left, he offered me a job and I accepted. He wanted to create a position for me as his special representative, who would teach his door-to-door salesmen how to put together a total sales presentation—the whole thing—how to use samples, how to dress, how to present yourself, how to clinch the sale. Everything.

Mr. Fuller wanted his employees, especially his salesmen, to present a certain image of success. He wanted the women who worked for him to drive big cars—either a Cadillac or a Lincoln—which had to be pink or white. Well, I drove up to Chicago from Louisville in my little Buick; and when he saw it, he laughed and said, "I think we can do better than that." At our first staff meeting, he made fun of me. He said, "Does anybody know whose little antique Buick with a Kentucky license plate is parked outside? If you do, let me know. I'd like for her to get a new car. If she needs any money, she can get it from my bookkeeper." Of course, he knew it was my car and he was having fun making his point. Everybody was laughing, and so was I.

When the meeting was over, the bookkeeper came to me and said, "Go see about a new car and let me know how much money you need." Well, I never wanted a Cadillac or a Lincoln in my life. To me, they were the cars that gamblers and preachers drove. But I went out to look at some big cars just to please Mr. Fuller. I was driving down the street, and in a show window I saw a sports model Plymouth in yellow, which I had always wanted. So I parked my car and went in to look at the Plymouth. While I was there, I saw also a Chrysler, which is a bigger car and which I also liked. I thought, well, this is a car I can live with and be proud of. I didn't buy either one right then but went back to my room.

The next day I continued car shopping and saw the same model Chrysler at another dealer. This time I bought it. I called a banker friend of mine at Liberty National Bank in Louisville and said, "I'm looking at a car here in Chicago that I want to buy. Will you tell this salesman that I am able to buy it?" So I put the salesman on, and the banker said, "Give this woman anything she wants. She can pay for whatever you've got. I will back her up." So I bought my blue Chrysler. But you know what? Mr. Fuller never said whether he liked it or not. He didn't say anything at all. Maybe he was miffed because I didn't follow his orders to the letter. I did not buy a Cadillac or a Lincoln for the simple reason that I did not like either one. If I was going to buy a new car for myself, I wanted it to be a car I liked—not the one Mr. Fuller liked! Of course, if he had bought one for me to use for the company, I would have driven it. But if I'm going to pay for it, I will decide which one to buy.

Mr. Fuller wanted his sales personnel to show off a certain image for Fuller Products, and he thought a big new car would do it. He didn't, however, specify what clothes we should wear. He could see, however, that he had nothing to worry about. We were all well-groomed, well-dressed and well-edu-cated men and women. After I had designed my model sales presentations and put together my sales kits, I tried them out on the salespeople in the Chicago area; then Mr. Fuller sent me to Detroit to instruct the dealers there. We had outlets in all the big towns in Illinois, Indiana, and Michigan.

Most of our cosmetics were for women, but we also sold a few items for men. We made and sold face creams, sham-poos, perfumes, lipstick, eye shadow, colognes, face powders, skin moisteners—everything for face makeup. We sold lotions and shaving creams and hair preparations for men. We may have sold skin lighteners, but I don't remember them, and I don't believe we sold hair straighteners. I do remember that we had solutions that would take the oil out of oily skin. Our products were designed for men and women of many differ-ent shades of color—from very dark to very light. We had prepa-rations for any complexion and any skin shade. Even white people could use our products. A friend of my second hus-band owned a radio station in Detroit, and I asked him to give me some air time to talk about cosmetics and makeup. One day I had a call from a club of young white women asking me to come to one of their meetings and bring my products. It was a great success. They were so impressed with my presen-tation that they bought all the products I had with me, and I had to go back for more. I don't know why they invited me to show our products to them. I was certainly surprised when I arrived and found a white group, but pretended not to be. In fact, it's been my policy never to act surprised at anything you see or anyone you meet. I've always gone along with it.

I was a good salesman, and every day after I finished my regular work demonstrating to Fuller salesmen how to sell the products, I went out to make my own house calls. I sold mainly to professional people of color on Boston Boulevard, which was a grand neighborhood of beautiful homes and cars. These

people were lawyers, doctors, dentists, ministers, business executives, and other professionals who could afford servants. It
was easy for me to sell $70 or $80 worth of cosmetics to one
customer's family. I was an early version of the Avon lady. I
did even better when I made sales presentations before clubs
and groups.

My approach was simple. I would demonstrate how to
apply the various facial preparations; then each person would
put on the cosmetics following my directions. Sometimes the
hostess would serve dinner following my presentation. It was
at one of those dinners that I was introduced to the delicious
little Cornish hens, which the husband of the hostess prepared.
Sometimes at those meetings I would clear $50 and more.
Actually, that wasn't hard to do if you had many buyers because the mark-up on cosmetics is very high. Salesmen weren't
paid straight salaries but were on commission, which usually
amounted to one-third of the sales price. In fact, my success
in selling cosmetics led to my leaving Fuller Products. I was
making so much money selling the products that the manager of the Detroit branch said to Mr. Fuller, "She's making
too much money. You're paying her a good salary, and now
she's making big money selling the cosmetics. Why don't you
reduce her salary?" Mr. Fuller was fool enough to do just that.
He cut $100 off my weekly salary. I couldn't believe I was again
being punished for doing a good job. I had agreed to work a
year for him, but I left after six months. I sent him a telegram
that said simply, "I am resigning my position as of today." It
surprised Mr. Fuller, but he did nothing to keep me on. His
wife told me she knew how jealous his employees were of me
and that she was very upset by the way I was being treated. But
I said, "Never mind. I can take care of myself. I've already got
a better position lined up. It's waiting for me right now."

Indeed I did. For the remaining six months on my leave
of absence I worked for Mr. Charles C. Diggs, who owned a
funeral home, an insurance company, and a flower shop as

well as a lot of other businesses in Detroit. I had met him a few weeks before and he had asked if I would run a campaign office for a friend of his who was running for the city council. Both Mr. Diggs and his son were very active in Democratic politics in Detroit and had served in the House of Representatives in Washington. So after I sent my telegram to Mr. Fuller, I called Mr. Diggs and said, "I'm ready to start working for you." He fixed up an office for me on a balcony overlooking his flower shop. I was in charge of the campaign finances and helped arrange the candidate's personal appearances — all from my office overlooking the flower shop. Just before the election I organized a big banquet as a grand finale to the campaign. It was just the final touch we needed, and our candidate was elected. Even during the victory celebration, however, there were people who made unkind remarks about me out of jealousy. They didn't like it that I was from Louisville and had handled the campaign of an important Detroit politician. Well, it was almost time for me to return to Louisville anyway. I had left Louisville in November and I returned in November. I remember the day I started home. It was a bright, beautiful fall day, and I was driving my handsome new Chrysler. I was ready to come home and resume my work here. I felt good. I spent the night with friends in Cincinnati, then drove on to Louisville the next day, where many of my neighbors were waiting to welcome me home.

Despite the petty jealousies I suffered, I enjoyed living in Chicago and Detroit. I discovered, however, that there was a lot of unofficial discrimination against blacks in the North. Even in those northern cities, it wasn't easy for blacks to find good places to stay. Legally, we could live anywhere we could afford, but in practice we were often excluded. In Chicago I lived with my friend, and in Detroit I got a room in a hotel that catered to blacks. Soon I met a schoolteacher who was living in nearby Dearborn, and she asked me to move in with her. I had my own bedroom, sitting room, and bath in her beautiful home across from a city park. Fortunately, I knew quite a few people in the black community in Chicago and Detroit before I moved up there.

People of color at certain levels used to know each other in towns and cities all over the country. Black lawyers, doctors, school principals, ministers, businessmen and women— we all knew our counterparts and colleagues in places like Chicago and Birmingham and Atlanta and Louisville. It was an unofficial network. It was therefore rather easy for us to find someone who would put us up when we arrived in a new city and needed a place to stay. But the fact is that I can live and be happy just about anywhere if I'm doing a job I like. That's all I've ever wanted: a good job where I'm treated fairly. The place is not important. When I move somewhere, I go there to work. I don't go there to play and goof off. I go there to work and do a good job. That's what's important to me. I don't have trouble working with anyone—male or female, young or old, white or black—if I'm treated right.

Unfortunately, the discrimination against blacks and against black professional women was everywhere. I certainly don't think that Mammoth ever treated me or my first husband right for the contributions we made. When Mr. Street died, he was holding down four positions, including treasurer, company secretary, and head of the claims department. When his position was filled, his jobs were then given to four men, and each one was paid his salary. Any way you look at it, it was not fair. Mammoth had let my husband work himself to death for the company and didn't reward him for it. Finally, I had to leave Mammoth because they continued to mistreat me. The men in the company—and even some of the women—were jealous of my success in every job I undertook to do. They were jealous of the good work I did, and I think they were jealous of the way I looked. I always looked nice. I always dressed well. I didn't have the money to buy a lot of expensive clothes and accessories, but I knew how to dress in good taste. I wasn't dressing to impress anybody. I wasn't trying to get a

better job. I looked the way I did because that was me. That
was the way I was. Whatever success I had came from my talents and my hard work.

After a few more years with Mammoth, I was growing very
tired and desperately needed a vacation because I had been
working so hard. I was so depressed I didn't work at anything
for three months. I didn't even look for a job. At that time Mr.
Kidd, my second husband, was still living and he supported
me. Before long, however, a Chicago insurance company,
Supreme Life, contacted me about becoming an agent for
them. They knew my good record at Mammoth and also my
work nationally in public relations. I took an eighteen-month
course in insurance underwriting at the University of Louisville, where I was one of two blacks and the only woman in
the class. I studied hard and learned a lot about the technicali-
ties of the insurance business. The other students called me
"Eager Beaver" because I was always asking questions and pok-
ing up my hand like a little child. Supreme Life paid for my
course and then challenged me to write a million dollars worth
of insurance. I didn't make that goal, but I wrote half a million, all in $35 and $45 policies to people in Louisville. I had
proved to everyone that I was still alive and well, but I was
getting tired of the insurance business and began to look for
greener pastures somewhere else. That's when I was drafted to
go into politics.

Despite the problems and prejudices I faced, the insurance business was good to me. I have never for a moment regretted my years of hard work at Mammoth. That company
did a lot for me. They gave me the opportunity to do things I
wanted to do. In return, I was always loyal to the company,
and I never tried to run it down. Even though I had been gone
from the company for many years, I was very sad when it was
sold and moved to Atlanta. It was a beautiful company. But
business is business, and you can't stop people from selling
their stock to the highest bidder.

Several years ago some people from North Carolina Mutual came to Mammoth and said, "We're here to buy this company. We want to take you over." Then Atlanta Life got in the act and said they would save the company. It became a price war. North Carolina Mutual offered $35 a share, and Atlanta countered with $40, and finally the bidding went up to $70. North Carolina dropped out. It turns out they were already in the red by $5 million, and they wanted Mammoth's assets in order to sell them off and pay their debts. Atlanta won the bidding and got the company. There was an attempt by Mr. James King, the president of Mammoth, to get stockholders to buy back their stock, but many of them were old people who needed that $70 a share. A person who had, say, 1,000 shares got a lot of money from his investment.

A lot of us who owned stock didn't realize earlier that if we sold our stock we might lose the company. So Mr. King's efforts failed, and Atlanta Life owned the company. We soon found out that Atlanta wasn't out to rescue the company. They needed Mammoth's assets too in order to pay off its debts. So they wound up doing what North Carolina was planning: they sold off our assets and closed the Louisville office. A few of the local employees went down to Atlanta to work, but Mammoth Insurance, a black-owned and operated company that so many of us worked so hard for and took so much pride in, is gone.

I cried when we lost the company. I had grown up with Mammoth—in Millersburg and in Louisville. I had a lot of my life invested in that company, and suddenly it was all gone. Except for a few years during World War II and a couple of years leave to pursue other business interests, I was with Mammoth from 1925 until 1966. A company founded in 1915 was suddenly gone. All the records were moved from Louisville to Atlanta, and the policies are being serviced by Atlanta Life. It's now all gone—as they say, it's all gone with the wind. I have very little to show for the forty years I worked at Mammoth—not even a pension. It wasn't until after I left in 1966 that the company began a pension plan for its employees. The company never even gave me any recognition for the work I did. Finally the Employees Credit Union honored me at a banquet and reception for organizing the union, which was then worth more than a quarter of a million dollars. You know, there are a lot of people who don't want you to succeed; and when you do, they don't want to give you credit for it.

Mammoth was one of more than seventy Negro insurance companies we used to have throughout the country. When these companies started, it was hard for blacks to buy insurance from white-owned companies. They didn't consider us good risks. The black-owned companies tried to serve a wide range of customers. A few companies like Metropolitan had what we called 10 cents insurance. My mother had three 10-cent policies, but they didn't amount to much. The death benefit was about $90. Such policies, however, gave thousands and thousands of black people a sense of security. The black insurance companies were truly a source of pride to many, many blacks.

Unfortunately, with integration in the 1950s and 1960s, the white companies began opening up their policies to blacks, and blacks deserted their own companies in droves. As usual, blacks turned their backs on their own color. They thought that the white man's insurance was somehow better than ours. What they didn't realize was that all the companies have to obey the same rules and regulations set up by the government.

It's sad but true that this desertion by blacks of black insurance companies is just a part of a larger problem in the black community: we just don't have enough confidence in our own people to patronize each other. There are enough blacks who have money that they could pool and build hotels and banks and other enterprises that would benefit not only the owners and investors but other blacks as well. Blacks have improved themselves a lot since I was a young woman, but we still don't believe in each other as much as we should. We're better educated and hold better positions in society and business. A lot of young blacks are being integrated into white companies. Overall, we're being accepted for what we can do and not shunned for our skin color. At the same time we are becoming more color-blind as a society, we blacks need to continue to help our own people.

We could learn a lot about helping ourselves from other ethnic groups like the Jews. They look out for each other. You hardly ever see a poor Jew. Jews help each other. Look at how successful Jewish Hospital here in Louisville has become. It's one of the most important hospitals in this part of the country. Blacks don't support each other and build up institutions like that. I am bothered a lot by our failure to unite and become a powerful economic force. I know it's partly the lack of self-esteem that is our legacy from slavery. We all started out in this country as slaves, and that's a terrible historical burden to have to carry. It robs us of our self-confidence. It makes us think of ourselves as permanent second-class citizens. We need to build on the pride that some of us now have in the role we played in the building of America. The Jews are proud of who they are—even though they were once slaves in Egypt—and call themselves God's Chosen People. Blacks must take a lesson from them.

My Two Husbands

I was never very popular as a girl or young woman. A lot of women were jealous of me, and a lot of men thought I was stuck-up. It's been a fact of my life that I've had to live with. I never intentionally did anything that I thought would make others jealous, and I never consciously behaved in a superior manner. I've only tried to live my life in a way that was meaningful to me. I had to live it my way. I've always wanted people to like and respect me, but I cannot control how other people see me.

Two good men loved me enough to ask me to be their wife. Yes, I had two husbands—Horace Leon Street, whom I married in 1930, and James Meredith Kidd III, in 1947. I have been widowed twice. Mr. Street died in 1942 and Mr. Kidd in 1972. I loved both of my husbands—indeed I did—but you know I could have gotten along without either one. I survived very well as a single woman until I was twenty-six years old, when I was first married. I didn't really need either one, but I have no regrets about my two marriages. Each one gave my life a new depth and dimension.

It wasn't until I was living in Louisville and in my twenties that I even had a serious boyfriend. In fact, my first serious boyfriend became my first husband, and he was thirteen years older than me. But the age difference was never a problem. I first met him in Lexington when he was speaking in a church, and I had come over from Millersburg to visit with some friends. Later he came with a Mammoth insurance supervisor to Millersburg. He said he had come to check up on business, but I think he really came to get acquainted with me. He found out where I lived and came by to see me. We had a pleasant visit, and as he was about to get into his car, he said, "Young lady, if you were older, I'd ask your mother if I could marry you. But you're too young for me." I was seventeen and I thought I'd never see him again. But our paths were fated to cross again. A few months later I became an agent for his company, and about four years later I came to Louisville to work in the home office where he was the company treasurer.

I liked Mr. Street well enough from the beginning, but I began to resent his meddling in my personal life. "Miss Jones," he'd say, "you know your mother would never approve of you doing this or going there or seeing so-and-so." I'd say, "Look, Mr. Street, you're not my father." One day he said, "Miss Jones, tomorrow is the company picnic. How would you like to ride with me in my car?" I said, "All right." We went with another couple and sat on a blanket and ate our food and played cards. After we got married, I said, "When you asked me to go to that picnic, you were just jivin' me, weren't you? But you got hooked!" After the picnic we started going out together regularly and became good friends. We'd go to a picture show at the Lyric Theater, which was located in the Mammoth Building, or we might have a picnic in Chickasaw Park. He liked to take me to dinners and receptions and show me off. He was tall, over six feet, and had a light-brown complexion. He dressed in the latest styles and always looked superb in his suit and straw hat. I liked the way he looked. He liked the way I looked. We made a stunning couple. About two years later we got married.

It happened one weekend on a visit to Millersburg. At work one day he said, "Mae, would you like to go see your mother?" I said I would. He picked me up in his car and we drove to Frankfort, where he said, "Would you like to stop and get a license to get married?" I said, "Are you proposing to me?" He said, trying to sound timid, "Yes, I suppose I am." After a little hesitation, I said yes, and we got the license in the court house, then drove on to my mother's home in Millersburg. He said to her, "Mrs. Taylor, we'd like to get married, and I've come to ask for your permission to marry your daughter. We already have the license." My mother, who never liked to be taken for granted, said, "Well, why did you get the license before you asked me?" That's all she said, but I could tell she was upset. We stayed there for the weekend, and by Sunday we still weren't married. Mr. Street began to get nervous and asked my stepfather for help. Finally, arrangements were made to have our Methodist preacher come to the house to marry us on Sunday afternoon in the living room. Mother still hadn't given us her blessing. In fact, she never said anything, but she later gave us a big reception. That was her way of saying, "Well, I don't like the way you did it, but I'll go along with it."

In Louisville we kept our marriage a secret for a while, but finally we announced it and received many beautiful gifts and invitations to dinners. We became a kind of golden couple in Louisville's black community. Soon after our marriage, we were invited by Mr. J. B. Smith, who was vice-president of Domestic Life Insurance Company, to his beautiful home on River Park Drive for Easter Sunday dinner. He had been an executive at Mammoth but had left to form Domestic, which became a competitor. Still, we were all friends and enjoyed socializing together. That Sunday I remember that Mr. Street and I both had on gray suits. Everyone complimented us on how stylish we looked together, and indeed we did.

Mr. Street was a native of Mayfield, Kentucky, and a graduate of Miles College, a Methodist school in Tennessee, where he studied to be a businessman. He was a very intelligent, nice-looking man. What impressed me the most, however, was his beautiful English. I have always been attracted to people who dress nicely and speak good English. Women always liked him because he behaved like a gentleman. As a top officer for Mammoth, he did a lot of traveling and met a lot of schoolteachers, especially on his trips around Kentucky. Well, some of these teachers would look him up when they came to Louisville for the Kentucky Negro Education Association meeting each year.

First husband, Horace Leon Street

He would take them out to lunch or for a ride in his car. After we had been going together about two years, I decided to put a stop to that activity. He had given me a key to his car, so I got in the car one day and drove it down here to this house where I had a room at the time. After a while, he called me and said, "Mae, I can't find my car. Do you know where it is?" I said, "Yes, I do. I've got it parked outside." He said, "Will you bring it to me?" I said, "No, I won't. I don't want you riding all these women schoolteachers around." When I finally took his car to him, it was too late for him to take his ladyfriends for a ride— at least that day. I knew he didn't like it, but he didn't say a critical word to me. And it broke his habit of flirting with those teachers.

When we married Mr. Street was thirty-nine years old and had never been married. I was twenty-six. I'd never even gotten close to marriage before. I would occasionally go to lunch or go driving or to a dance with a male friend, but that was all. People thought I had a lot of boyfriends because I was so attractive. I didn't. If I had pushed myself, however, I could have found a husband earlier, but I didn't see anyone I wanted. I never cared about being popular. I didn't flirt with men, and I didn't want them flirting with me. If it took flirting to be popular, I wanted none of it. If I had a relationship with a man, I wanted it to be serious.

Of course, another thing I liked about Mr. Street was his car. I had learned to drive a little soon after I came to Louisville, but, of course, I couldn't afford my own car. While he and I were going together, we often went on drives in his car. Sometimes he would let me drive it, and one day I decided I would try it all by myself. He had already given me a key to the car, so I borrowed it from the parking lot at Mammoth and drove it around until I felt confident. He didn't say a word when he discovered what I had done. Before and after our marriage, I would help drive on long trips. Soon after we married, he wanted to drive to St. Louis to show me off to an uncle and some cousins, and I drove most of the way there and back.

I have always enjoyed driving and having a car. Back then, a lot of women didn't care about driving and didn't know how. Their husbands or fathers or brothers or some other relative had to take them when they wanted to go someplace. I didn't care for that kind of dependence. Driving—especially driving my own car—has always made me feel independent. It's given me a sense of freedom. It's a good thing for a woman to own a car and to own a home. It makes her feel like somebody. If you've got a roof over your head, you don't feel you have to bow and scrape to anybody. If you have your own house and your own car as well, then you're your own person. The car

especially is your pal. It's your friend who takes you places anytime you want to go. Even though I can't drive it anymore, I
still have my car parked outside in the garage. It's a big silver
Chrysler Fifth Avenue, the top of the line.

Before we bought this house, we lived in an apartment in
the Mammoth Building. That's where we were living during
the 1937 flood. It was a busy, hectic time for all of us. The
water didn't reach our building at Sixth and Muhammad Ali,
but we were anxious about our friends in sections of the West
End that were under water. Our good friends, the James B.
Smiths, lived out in a flooded area. I called him and said,
"What are you all still doing there?" He said, "What do you
mean? We're all right. The water is coming up now through
the furnace ducts, but we're not wet yet." I said, "Man, you
listen here. You put some things in a suitcase and get in a boat
and come up here to our apartment. We're up high enough to
be safe unless the flood covers all of Kentucky and Indiana.
Now if you don't come on down here, I'll call the police and
tell them there are some crazy people living at your address."
That convinced them to leave, but it took all day for them to
get to our apartment.

Mr. Street and I had a comfortable apartment but only
one bedroom. Fortunately, we had a couch in the living room
that made into a bed, and I turned that room into their bedroom. It was close quarters but we made out. It's a good thing
we were such good friends because they stayed with us for six
weeks. The men were able to go downstairs to the street level
and pick up food that was being delivered by the Red Cross.
There was also a handy grocery store right across the street
that stayed open. We stayed busy cooped up all day, listening
to the radio reports, reading, playing bridge, and talking on
the telephone. We stayed there throughout the flood and the
clean-up.

One day we had a notice that the building was getting too
full of people, and officials started going door-to-door to see
how many were staying in each apartment. When they got to

our door, I said, "My husband and I are just fine." I didn't mention that the Smiths were living with us and that they were just fine too. I'm sure if they had found the Smiths, they would have forced them to a shelter. Except for the inconvenience of being cooped up for so long, the flood didn't bother us much. But living so close for so long to my husband and my friends was certainly a test for marriage and friendship.

Mr. Street died of heart disease in 1942, when he was only forty-nine. We were living in this house by then, and my half sister and half brother were living with us. She and I nursed him at home for over a year during his illness, right up to his death. I was working at Mammoth, but I had permission to report for work each morning after I'd taken care of Mr. Street's needs. When my sister came in from school early in the afternoon, she took care of him. He had a telephone by his bed and could call me if he needed to. He was a good patient, easy to take care of even though he was very sick for a long time. He was constantly thanking us for being so nice to him. A few weeks before his death, my mother came over to help us tend him. We also had a nurse that we could use when necessary. The doctor wanted to move him to a hospital, but he didn't want to go, and I didn't want him to go. I said, "Honey, you're going to stay here in your home." And he did. I never did trust doctors or hospitals too much. You're always having to look over their shoulders to make sure they don't make a mistake. At home you can make sure things are done right.

A childhood friend of his from Mayfield came to be with him just before he died. Just before the end, she came to me and said, "Mae, you go downstairs and get some rest. I'll watch by his bedside." In less than an hour she came down to say that he had just passed. It was an agonizing trial for me to go through. It was so painful for me to see him so sick and in so much suffering. But I was consoled by the fact that he died at home in his bed in our bedroom surrounded and cared for by those who loved him. He had a beautiful funeral service at the C.M.E. Church.

After Mr. Street's death, I had to go my way alone. I think I surprised a lot of people with what I could do. Of course, people knew that I was active in the YWCA, the USO, my church, and other organizations, but they didn't know how well I could do without my husband. They had forgotten that I had been single most of my life and had survived very well. But while I was married, I hadn't really asserted myself. I was Mrs. H. L. Street. I was Mr. Street's wife and hostess. Once I got over the sorrow of his death, I began to spread my wings and fly. It was almost as if his death freed me to develop my talents and interests. Before long, I had volunteered to do work with the Red Cross, and after that the United Seamen's Service, and I became an independent, successful woman in several careers. I learned to make the most of the opportunities I had.

I met my second husband, James Meredith Kidd III, in Southampton, England, in 1944, when I was working with the Red Cross and he was an army officer. It was a typical wartime romance, and when I left to return home we were engaged. He had studied at Wayne State University in his hometown of Detroit and had taught in a black school in Charleston, West Virginia, before he went into the service. When the war in Europe was over, he was transferred to the Philippines, and was on his way home when V-J Day was declared. He wired me from his troopship the date and time he would be arriving in Chicago by train. I was so excited that I flew to Chicago and surprised him by meeting him at his train. He went on to his home in Detroit, where his family lived as the only black family in a Polish neighborhood called Hamtramck. His father was a physician and very respected by his white patients.

Although we didn't get married for a couple of years, he made frequent trips to Louisville to see me. Finally, we were married at the Woodlawn A.M.E. Church in Chicago on August 20, 1947. We had our wedding night in Kankakee Shores, Illinois, and then went to Detroit to pick up his brother's car for our honeymoon to Quebec, Canada, and Niagara Falls.

Second husband, James Meredith Kidd III

After he got out of the army, he went to law school for a while, but he didn't finish. I think he was like a lot of soldiers. He got confused being in the army and then coming back to be a civilian. He had trouble adjusting. Even after we married, we lived separately for over a year. He had a good job in Detroit, and I had my job in Louisville. Then one time he was visiting me and met Mr. J. B. Smith, my friend who was vice-president of Domestic Life Insurance Company, who offered him a job, which he accepted. Almost from the beginning he didn't like the job. You know, sometimes it's hard for smart people to get settled and satisfied. It's hard for them to get to the place where they want to be — or *think* they want to be. So he started taking courses at Louisville Municipal Col-

Picture she sent overseas to Kidd

With James Meredith Kidd on their honeymoon

lege to get a teaching certificate. When he finished, he got a
job for a year in Paris, Kentucky, where my sister lived. This
was in the early fifties about when the schools were being integrated.

The following summer he was taking some summer school
courses, and the supervisor of science classes for the Louisville City Schools called him and asked if he would like to
teach science at Shawnee Junior High. The supervisor said,
"You have just the qualifications we want. You have a good
academic record. You attended integrated schools in Michigan. You would be a good choice to teach mixed classes of
blacks and whites." He took the job, and that pleased me very
much because he could live at home with me all the time.

Yes, Kidd, as I called him, was a brilliant man, and I like
brilliant men. But I did divorce him. Not many people know
I've been divorced because I'm a very private person. I don't
go around broadcasting my personal life. I don't put my busi-

ness out in the street. To tell the truth, I don't really know why I left him. I suppose I just didn't like some of his ways. He had some habits I couldn't take. Let's leave it at that. I was engrossed in my work at Mammoth, and our domestic problems interfered with my work. And I don't like for anything to interfere with my work. So about five years after we married, we divorced. We were not angry and bitter at each other. We were always fond of each other. He always said I was a lady. "If I've ever known a lady, Mae," he said, "you are the one."

Now here's the funny part. We were only divorced for a few months, and I had to go to California on a business trip. When I got back, he called me and we talked about our relationship. "Will you come back to me, Mae, and give me another chance?" he pleaded. Finally I said I would, and we got back together. We went over to Indiana and married again and were still married when he died.

In many ways Kidd was a very sad, unhappy person. He was a searcher, but I don't think he ever found what he was looking for. He came close to his true vocation in teaching, and perhaps he was happiest when he was with his students. I still meet some of his old students from Shawnee, and they say proudly, "I went to school under Mr. Kidd." I say, "Well, what kind of teacher was he? Was he mean?" And they say, "Oh no, ma'am, he wasn't mean, but he was strict. When we were noisy, he'd tell us to pipe down. And sometimes he'd walk down the aisles with his elbows sticking out and bump us if we were not in our seats. Then he'd say, 'Oh excuse me, I must have bumped you.' Then everybody would laugh and get down to business." Yes, I think teaching was as close as he ever got to finding his place in life. The good memories that I have of him and Mr. Street make the end of my life pleasant. There are no perfect matches in this world, but my two husbands came close.

The House and Street
Where I Live

I love my home. It is a sacred place to me. When Mr. Street and I got married in early 1930, he was living with a family on Eighth Street; and I was renting a room in this very house from a Mrs. Mahin. We moved into an apartment on the fifth floor of the Mammoth Building, where we both worked, and lived there until we bought this house in 1938. It was just after Christmas in 1937, and I was in New York attending a convention of Iota Phi Lambda, my businesswomen's sorority, with a friend of mine. When I arrived home, Mr. Street told me that Mrs. Mahin had just been killed in an automobile accident and that her house was for sale. He said, "You've always liked that house. Would you like to have it?" I said, "Yes, I certainly would." Then he said kind of vaguely, "Well, I'll see about it."

A few nights later we were sitting in the living room of our apartment talking and he said, "When do you want to go down and look at our new house and see what repairs and redecorating we need to do? And when do you want to move?" I said, "Move? Move where?" He said, "Oh, I bought that house on Chestnut Street." I said, "Well, it sounds good, but I haven't seen the deed." He said, "I have it." I said, "Whose name is on it?" He said, "Mine." I thought a minute and then said, "Well, I'll tell you what. I'll give you two weeks to add my name to that deed; and if you don't, not only will I not live in that house with you, but I'll not live with you anywhere." You know what? It didn't take that man two weeks to put me in joint ownership

73

of the house. Two days later he stopped by my desk and said, "Mrs. Street, we have an appointment tomorrow to see the lawyer to change the deeds."

Believe me, but I didn't mean to sound greedy. I knew I had to look out for my interests. After all, something could happen to him anytime, and I would be left high and dry. I also felt that I deserved an interest in the house that we were going to share as man and wife. It's a good thing I did. Not long after we moved in, he became very sick and couldn't go to the annual meeting of the National Negro Insurance Association in Birmingham and make his report as national treasurer. He asked me to go in his place. In my absence his sister from St. Louis came over to stay with him. Well, you know the devil starts working the minute your back is turned. When I returned I found out that while his sister was here, she began to work on him to make her the beneficiary of a $1,500 insurance policy. She worried him and worried him until he agreed to make the change. That really upset me. Here was a sick man on his death bed, and his own sister was pestering him behind his wife's back for part of his estate.

But she still wasn't satisfied. Then she began to complain to me that she didn't have a share in our house. She and I were sleeping together in the same bed, and she was keeping me awake griping half the night. Finally, I had to get up and sleep on the chaise lounge to get away from her. But I found a way to have the last word. When he died, I told the undertaker's secretary to attach the policy to pay the funeral bill. That way his greedy sister didn't get a penny!

Yes sir, you have to look out for yourself in this world because people will run over you if they're given half a chance. Nobody else is going to do it for you. Most people will try to take advantage of you if they can. If you are sharp, you can handle it. And don't expect all the sharpsters to be down the street or from out of town. Your own relatives will fleece you clean. Some of my own family have questioned my plans to establish a scholarship fund with my estate, but there's noth-

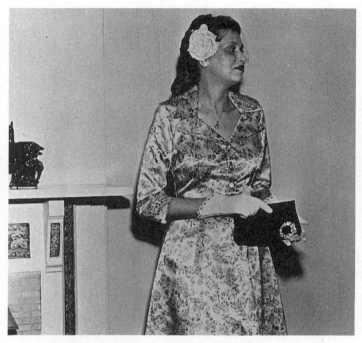

Preparing for a night out in her home on Chestnut Street

ing they can do. It's all settled. This is the way it is. You work hard all your life for your money, and nobody in your family will lift a hand to help you. But wait until they smell some money, and they put in their claim just like they deserve it.

Now, I'll get down off my soapbox and tell you about my house and show you why I treasure it so much. When this house was built in the 1880s by a German family, it was on an all-white street of well kept middle-class homes. It has gradually become one of the finest black neighborhoods in Louisville. The house is a classic Federal design and has seven large rooms and an unfinished third floor. I don't know the name of the German who built it, but I've been told that the vinework on my living room mantel piece is a German design. Incidentally, I have fireplaces in every room except the kitchen, which has a gas stove. All the beautiful woodwork and the original

House on Chestnut Street

stained glass windows throughout the house are also charac-
teristic of the Germans.

Now let me take you on a tour of my house. I think it'll
show you why I'd rather be here than in a nursing home! First,
the living room, where I have a grand piano. No, I don't play.
I bought it for my sister, Mary Evelyn Taylor, when she was
thirteen and living with me. She took lessons and learned to

Chestnut Street today

play very well. Across the hall is the family room, which was originally the dining room. When we moved here, my husband asked me if I wanted a dining room set, and I said I did not. It's the most expensive furniture you buy for your house, and it's for a room that's seldom used. So we made it into a family room. When we had company for dinner and needed more eating space, I just moved in a table with leaves. All three of my bedrooms are on the second floor, including one with a sitting room, which I used to rent out to celebrity guests. I'll tell you about them later.

When we bought this house, there were some features I didn't like—such as doors opening into every room. So we took many of the doors down and put in archways that make the downstairs look like a California house. A feature I did like was the tall ceilings, almost eleven feet high. They give an air of spaciousness to the rooms, but if they were any taller it would be too expensive to heat and cool them. They are just the right size.

The other big room downstairs is my kitchen, which is painted in blue, pink, and white. You'll notice that the sink is unusual. It's huge—seventy-two inches long—and it took five men to install it. It's been in this house for fifty-four years. The gas range next to the sink came from Sears Roebuck. On top it has an oven and four burners, and at the bottom is space for cooking utensils. That range is the centerpiece for the kitchen. People marvel over it and can't believe it's 54 years old. It looks good as new because I've taken good care of it. In fact, I've taken care of my entire house. Mother, you may remember, never let me do domestic work for other people, but she taught me how to keep my own house. Until I lost my eyesight, I did most of my own house work because I wanted everything spotless; and the best way to make sure it was done the way I wanted it was to do it myself.

If you want to know what kind of housekeeper a person is, check out her stove. I always keep my stove immaculate. The Sears, Roebuck people tell me they don't keep stove parts more than ten years because they want you to buy a new one. I asked Sears about two years ago to send a man out here to do a minor repair on my stove, and as soon as he got inside the back door, he said, "Aw, that's an old stove. It's no good." I said, "What do you mean about it being old and no good? Doesn't it look good?" He said, "Yes ma'am. But we don't carry parts for a model that old." Then he went over and began to examine it closely and said, "Mrs. Kidd, since you've kept it up so nice for so long, I'll try to find the parts and come back and fix

In her (spotless) kitchen

it." You know what? He did find the parts and fixed my stove, and now it's as good as new.

We left intact the old cabinets because I like the idea of an antique kitchen. I did have the glass doors replaced with wooden ones painted mint green. I didn't want people to see through the doors. It's hard to keep dishware nice and straight, and I didn't want a mess visible through the glass.

You've probably noticed that I like a lot of color in my house. My favorite color is dusty rose, and I used it in several rooms. When you sit in this kitchen, you can look through the doorway out into the hall and see the steps with the red carpet going upstairs. You can see my wallpaper with its urns and flowers. Oh, but it's a beautiful sight! When you look into the den, you can see more flowers on the wallpaper. I paid a premium price for that paper at Hubbuch & Wellendorf, one of Louisville's finest interior design shops. It has a classical look to it. I have it cleaned every two years because I can't find a good replacement.

This is as good a place as any to make a small confession. I love my house and I'm proud of the way it looks. I try to keep it spotless and shining. But there are many of the details of housekeeping I don't really care about. Take cooking, for instance. I cooked when I had to, but I was never too thrilled about it. If I didn't have to cook, I didn't cook. But if I had to cook, I did it right. Another household job I've never relished is sewing. It's a slow and unrewarding chore. One time I made a very attractive dress for myself, and I was so proud of it I had my picture made in it.

Let's go outside through the kitchen door into the back yard. You will notice a beautiful concrete patio with wrought iron tables and chairs. My husband and I used to sit out here and entertain our company.

Aren't you impressed with my yard? I did the landscaping myself. I have thick bluegrass all over the ground. I used to do most of my own yard work. At one time I had more than forty rose bushes of many varieties that bloomed from spring into the fall. Some of them had stems up to twenty-two inches long. People would walk and drive by just to see my roses. Every spring I would replace the ones I lost during the cold winters. I have a man who does my yard work now, but I'm sad to say he doesn't do a very good job.

You haven't said anything about my garage! For a long time, I didn't have a garage. My car got hit twice because I had to park it on the street. First, I built a concrete slab behind the house so I could park the car on my own property. About eight years ago I built the garage over the slab. It's made of wood and brick and looks just like a little house and it's big enough for a little dance or a barbecue. Around the garage I have spider lilies and lilacs and irises. All around the yard I have many annuals and tulips and jonquils. It's a beautiful sight when they're all blooming.

I've never worried much about security and safety here in my house. I've always felt safe and I've never had a break-in. I added a burglary alarm when I went away to serve in the General Assembly in Frankfort in 1968 because I would be gone for the entire week while the legislature was in session. Later, I installed a floodlight in the back yard. Nobody on this street, to my knowledge, has ever had a break-in. We look out for each other's property. If someone's alarm goes off while they're gone, a neighbor will call the police. When my own alarm sometimes rings falsely, my phone starts ringing. "Mrs. Kidd," the neighbors say, "is that your alarm? Are you all right?" Yes, indeed, I feel safe here, even at my age and in my condition.

Before I tell you about this wonderful neighborhood called Chestnut Street, I'll share with you some of the celebrities who have rented rooms in my house over the years. Until the early 1960s it was impossible for blacks—even the big-name celebrities—to stay at the big downtown Louisville hotels. Since I had a large, comfortable house, I was often asked to keep them while they were in town. I set up the front bedroom on the second floor as a special room for my guests. It was a combination sitting room and bedroom, with an alcove where the bed was located. The room also had a fireplace and a television set. I never had to advertise. People knew I had a nice home and that occasionally I would let the right class of person stay with me. I was very selective. I wouldn't take in any Tom, Dick, or Jane.

I'll name just a handful of the better-known people who stayed at 2308 Chestnut Street and begin with Roy Wilkins, who was national director of the Urban League. He happened to be staying here the night my sister graduated from high school. After her graduation ceremony, she went to a party with some of her friends and then called me to pick her up. Mr. Wilkins and I were talking in my living room when she called, and he said, "May I go with you? I'd like to see how young people celebrate their graduation." He went with me and had a chance to talk to a number of her friends. He complimented them and encouraged them to continue their education and make their parents proud of their success.

A name you may not know now is Philippa Duke Schuyler. She was a piano prodigy in the 1940s and 1950s. Her father was a black man and her mother was German. While still a young woman, she became an outstanding pianist and composer and performed all over the world. By the time she was eight she had written more than fifty compositions. When she was twelve, her first symphonic composition, *Manhattan Nocturne*, was performed at Carnegie Hall. Later her works were performed by the Boston Pops and the New York Philharmonic. Unfortunately, she became a war correspondent and got killed on the battlefield in Vietnam. Her young life was wasted on that war that wasted so many lives.

I was her hostess twice, in 1941 and in 1959, when she played at Memorial Auditorium. I remember that her mother, who traveled with her, insisted that she eat only natural and raw foods—no sugar or baked breads. She brought with her a basket of food and made a bread of figs, dates, egg yolk, melted butter, whole wheat flour, and honey. For breakfast, I served her cottage cheese, grape juice, and tuna fish with lemon juice. Each time she came I knew I had to lay in a large supply of fresh fruits and vegetables. Actually, she was easy to feed because she ate them all raw. What a magnificent talent she had at the piano! And what a loss when she died so young. Not many people remember her today.

A person who is still remembered is Eddie "Rochester" Anderson, Jack Benny's sidekick and manservant on radio and television and in the movies. He, his wife, and his valet all stayed with me in 1943, when he ran a horse named Burnt Cork in the Kentucky Derby. I sat in his box and saw the horse come in tenth. I liked his wife very well because she was friendly and wanted to mingle with Kentucky people, but I didn't care anything at all for Rochester. He seemed too stand-offish and even tried to leave without paying me. I let them have two bedrooms on my second floor, and Rochester would drag his luggage down the steps and treat my house like it was a hotel. Finally, I said, "Now look here, this is not a hotel. This is my home, so treat it like one." The fact that he was a celebrity didn't cut any mustard with me. I judge people by how they behave, not by their name or money.

Now I'll tell you about my neighborhood. People on Chestnut Street may not visit and sit on each other's front porches like we did in Millersburg when I was a girl, but we are friendly and check on each other. I have lived a very active life and haven't had a lot of time to sit and gossip, but my neighbors have always known I was here when they needed me.

Chestnut Street is still a good place to live, but it's not quite what it used to be. When I came to Louisville, beautiful people lived all up and down this street. They were professional people—doctors and insurance men and ministers and business executives and lawyers and postal employees and teachers and undertakers. My next door neighbor for a long time was a well-to-do undertaker. We also had well-paid porters and waiters on this street. The head waiter at the Brown Hotel lived across the street from this house. He was one of the best-paid working men in Louisville—white or black. He made a lot of money from tips given him by rich white people that he served at the Brown Hotel. He was a smart dresser and had the biggest car on the block. Railroad porters made a lot of money then too, especially if they served on long-distance trains, like from New York to California. After the war I noticed that many of the porters during the summers were young black men who were working to pay their college expenses in medical or law school. They were fine young people who worked hard to accumulate something.

The people on this street were well known in the churches

With Eddie "Rochester" Anderson, his wife, valet, and others

and lodges of this town. They lived in brick homes, surrounded by well-kept yards, which you can still see if you drive around this neighborhood. You could say that the Who's Who of Black Louisville lived on Chestnut Street—the cream of our society.

Most of the poorer blacks—like garbage collectors and cooks and yardmen and maids—lived on other streets, and then when the housing projects were built, they moved into them. At one time Beecher Terrace, which was one of our first housing projects in Louisville, was a beautiful, well-kept place to live, and many successful men and women grew up there. They had a spacious social hall for dances and card parties and dinners.

We still have a very fine street, though I see a couple of houses that have been boarded up. That looks bad, but I can't do anything about it. Everybody used to keep their property up, but now we're losing pride of ownership. Nevertheless, we still have a lot of good professional people on this street. Next door to me is Betty Bayé, who is an associate editor of the *Cou-*

rier-Journal, and next door to her is a retired schoolteacher named McHenry. She bought a duplex and is fixing it up so that when she gets older and sick she can have someone come and live with her in a private part of the house. Like so many of us women who now live on this street, Mrs. McHenry is a widow. Another close neighbor is Minor Daniels, who keeps track of delinquent children for the Board of Education.

A lot of us old-timers still choose to live here in preference to other parts of town. I know a few people who have moved into the white neighborhoods in the East End; and I know quite a few blacks who have moved into the 800 Apartments, a high-rise downtown which was formerly all-white. A friend of mine said to me several years ago, "Mae, why don't you move to Eastern Louisville so you can live in a better neighborhood?" I said, "What do you mean, 'better neighborhood?' I love this street and these people. I'm happy where I am. I don't have a special wish to live with any color of people — white, black, green, or blue. I just want a decent neighborhood, and that's what we have here. Anyway, honey, I don't want another mortgage." Indeed, I have no desire to live anywhere but right here on Chestnut Street. I hope I draw my last breath on this street in this house.

Service Abroad

When World War II came on, I wanted to do something to help the war effort; but my first husband was already sick, and I had to stay close to him. It wasn't until after his death in 1942 that I could make a significant contribution as an overseas Red Cross volunteer. At the beginning of the war, however, I helped organize a USO at the old YMCA at Tenth and Chestnut in Louisville. We had a group of more than 150 women and girls who served and entertained the black soldiers from Fort Knox. When I was asked to be chairman, I said, "I'm sorry, but I have a very sick husband and don't have the time." The nominating committee said my main job would be to preside at meetings and be a public spokesman for the organization. Committees would do most of the work. "You serve as chairman of our meetings, and we'll do everything else," they said. Under those conditions, I agreed to head the USO.

One of our projects was to beautify the banquet hall on the top floor of the old Y building. We made drapes and repaired and painted and cleaned to make it a beautiful place to entertain black soldiers when they were in town on leave. We had dances every weekend and served food and nonalcoholic refreshments. We didn't do anything very elaborate, but the soldiers were so pleased to have some place to go when they left the camp. We had stationery and pens and tables where they could write letters home, and we had women who would write letters for men who couldn't write very well. Most places of entertainment were off-limits to black soldiers, and the black-run night spots were too expensive for many of them. The black

With USO volunteèrs in Louisville

clubs could sometimes be very rough. Most of the soldiers had to be back to camp by eleven or twelve o'clock, but we did have a few rooms at the Y where they could spend the night. We also rented two buses to take our women volunteers to Fort Knox to serve as hostesses and dance with the soldiers on base.

Another of our USO projects was to host special speakers and entertainers. One time when Marian Anderson came to Louisville to perform at Memorial Auditorium, we took her out to Fort Knox to do a concert. She had the most wonderful voice. As chairman of our USO, I rode next to her in the car to the camp, and she was sweet and gracious to me. She did a concert for all the soldiers—not just the black ones—and everybody was so excited to have her there, I think they forgot to segregate the audience!

My work with the USO indirectly led to my work with the Red Cross. A man named Jesse Thomas came from the Red Cross headquarters in Washington to Kentucky to recruit workers and stopped at Kentucky State College for Negroes in Frankfort. The president of the college, Dr. Rufus Atwood, said, "There's a woman in Louisville who's just lost her husband that would do a good job for you. She's active in USO work and knows how to take charge and manage people." It was a Sunday afternoon, and I was sitting here alone when the phone rang. Dr. Atwood said, "Mrs. Street, my friend Jesse Thomas is here from Washington to recruit women to work for the American Red Cross. Since you are already active in the USO, I thought you might like to talk with him." I said, "Send him over. I'll talk with him." My husband had just died, and I needed to get away for a while.

While I was waiting for Mr. Thomas to arrive later that afternoon, I said to myself, "What am I going to talk to this man about? Well, I'll just tell him what we do with the USO here in Louisville." So I told him about the 150 women volunteers we had recruited to help entertain soldiers from Fort Knox. That was apparently what he wanted to hear because about a week later I had a wire from the Red Cross asking me to come to Washington for another interview. I had told Mr. Thomas that I was not interested in being a coffee and doughnut girl. "If you want to make me a doughnut girl," I told him, "I won't come." He assured me that my qualifications were good enough for a higher kind of work. So I decided to go to Washington to see what they had in mind.

When I arrived in Washington, I called his office and made an appointment. The first person I saw was an elderly lady who had worked for the Red Cross a long time. She said my interviews would take two days and involve several people, and she promised they would not make me a doughnut girl. During my interview with her, I let her do the talking about Red Cross work. That impressed her, and she turned me over to the next person. Everything went smoothly and I was finally sent back to the first woman, who said, "Now you are in the Red Cross, Mrs. Street. Can you get your affairs in order and report for work in two weeks?" I said, "No, I cannot come in two weeks because I have a lot of business to take care of. I have a house to empty and rent. I have to store my furniture. I have ten tons of coal in my basement to sell. And I have a lot of other things

Being presented gifts at a YMCA good-bye party

to do. No, I cannot be here in two weeks. Anyway, I'm not sure I have any guarantees. What if I come back and you decide not to take me? I'll be in a bad situation. I will have lost everything. But I'll go home and see if I can get my business in order, and then I'll notify you." She said, "That's all right. We like you and we know we want you to work for us. You can come when you are ready and we'll have a position for you. Just let us know when to expect you." I said, "I'll let you know."

After I got home to Louisville, I called my mother in Millersburg and she helped me store my furniture in Paris, Kentucky, which was nearby. This sudden change in my life began to upset me. I cried every day. I didn't think I wanted to go because it was a big risk, but I knew the change would be good for me. It seemed the right time for me to launch out into the unknown. My husband had just died. My sister, who was living with me, had just left for college. My brother was in

the service. Four of us had been living in this house, and now
I was alone and lonesome. I remember sitting at this very
kitchen table on Sunday morning and crying. I was still working at Mammoth as supervisor of policy issue, but alone I didn't
make enough money to maintain this house. My career was
stalled, and I was bored with my work. I knew in my heart that
I needed a fresh start. I needed to get as far away from all my
sadness as I could, and I knew there was a good possibility that
I would be sent overseas. I knew, therefore, that the Red Cross
was offering me a good opportunity to serve my country while
I was healing my wounds.

After I stored my furniture, I rented my house to a minister, and all I had to do was sell my car. I was staying with my
friends, the J. B. Smiths, and I ran an ad in the paper for my
Buick. It was a car that I had dearly enjoyed and loved, and I
hated to part with it. But it had to be done because I couldn't
take it with me. The man who bought the car drove me to the
bank to get the money. After we got under way, I said, "Be
careful not to get too close to the curb and scratch my tires
and fenders." Then I remembered and said, "Oh, I'm sorry.
It's your car now." He laughed and said, "Don't worry, Mrs.
Street. I'll take good care of your car." By that time, the tears
were rolling down my cheeks. I had just sold the last thing
that represented my old life in Louisville and in Kentucky,
and I didn't know what I was getting into. It was going to be a
big change in my life, and I didn't know whether I could adjust to it. It was the biggest challenge I had ever faced.

I have never liked a quitter, and I was determined to go
through with my decision. After I got back to Washington, I
stayed with other black women who were being trained for
Red Cross work in a dormitory at Howard University. We went
to classes and on field trips around Washington every day to
learn how to do Red Cross work. One time we went down to
the Agriculture Department to observe how they prepared and
served food to large numbers of people. At the end of the training period of several weeks, we took an exam.

In her American Red Cross uniform

I had done so well with the training and on the exam that I was given the job of supervising the Loft at American University in Washington. The Loft was a social club where we served both black and white Red Cross trainees. I was put in charge of a mixed group of seven black and white Red Cross workers. It was the first time I had ever supervised white people. At first, I was a little nervous, but I soon got used to it. We remodeled the club to make it more comfortable and attractive. We painted the walls in bright, cheerful colors, put up pictures, and replaced the worn-out furniture. Everyone was so impressed with the dramatic change. Someone said, "Believe it or not, a woman from Louisville; Kentucky, is responsible for all this work." I was pleased because I had proved that I could get things done in my new job.

I had only one problem while I was supervisor. It involved a white girl, but it was not a racial incident. I had posted the duty schedules for the seven Red Cross workers, and the girl came to me and said, "I'm sorry, but I can't work Tuesday afternoon because I'm having my hair shampooed and set." I said, "I'm sorry too, but aren't you being paid for working here?" She said yes and I said, "Well, the Red Cross is not paying you to have your hair done on their time. You will have to work as scheduled." She said, "I won't be there. I'm going to have my hair done." I said, "Well, we'll see."

When the director came, I told her about the problem and asked if I'd done anything wrong. She said, "No, indeed not. You did the right thing. Call a meeting of all the women." At the meeting she said, "Ladies, I want you to get this straight. Please understand that Mrs. Kidd is supervisor here. You will have to do what she says do." Well, that nipped any revolt against my authority in the bud. The young woman did not get her hair done on Tuesday. She worked as she was scheduled to work. I don't believe my color was a factor at all. I don't think she resented me because I was black and had authority over her. I don't even know whether she realized I was black. In fact, I was as white as she was. I think she simply thought she could get away with doing anything she wanted. Some of the other women felt the same way, but after our meeting there were no further problems. If I had not put my foot down, I could have had problems with all of them. I learned that a good manager stops problems before they get big.

Before long, however, I did have a race-connected problem. I was scheduled to return to Kentucky and recruit young black women for the Red Cross, but someone on the selection committee objected. She said I would not be a good recruiter of black women. Guess why not? She said, "Mrs. Kidd is too white. Nobody will believe that she's black." Imagine that! A woman of my color was always having problems, but this was a new one. I was too white for this situation, and I was too black for that one. I argued that I could easily pass for black, but the committee wouldn't send me. Instead, I stayed in Washington and continued my training for overseas duty at American University.

A couple of months later I got a notice to come to a meeting where I would be assigned my overseas duty station. We couldn't choose where we would be sent. The Red Cross could send us anywhere, and I began to get nervous. I knew I did not want to go to the Philippines or anywhere in the South Seas, where the climate was too hot and steamy. I decided to scout around to see if I could find out where we were to be sent. I knew that our new uniforms would indicate the climate, so I went down to the supply room to see what I could see. I asked the clerk, "What kind of clothing will we be issued for the new assignments?" She said, "Oh, Mrs. Kidd, I'm not supposed to show you." I said, "Well, all right." As I turned to leave, I saw a pile of uniforms on the counter near the door, and I took a peep. Seersucker! Hot weather clothes! That meant somewhere in the South Seas!

It depressed me to think that I might have to spend a year in some sweaty jungle. I had to get my orders changed. So I bought a box of candy and went back to the dormitory room at Howard and called Mr. Jesse Thomas, the man who had recruited me. I said, "Mr. Thomas, I've just heard some bad news. I've been assigned to go overseas, and I understand that our uniforms will be seersucker. That means we're going to a tropical area, and I am not going." He said, "I'm sorry but you'll have to go where you are sent." I said, "Did you hear what I said? I'm not going." He said, "All right. I'll see what I can do about it."

The next day when I went to the meeting for the overseas assignments, one of the Red Cross officials came over to me and said, "Mrs. Street, you don't have to be here. We've changed your assignment. You'll go on the next trip that comes up." I said, "Thank you" and went back to my room, greatly relieved. Later, a young woman who had just returned from an assignment in Alaska came to my room and said, "I'm going to the Philippines. I've heard you're not going. I don't understand why they changed your orders." I smiled and didn't say anything, but I gave her the rest of my box of candy.

Then I had the misfortune of having an attack of pleurisy, which I hadn't fully recovered from when the next overseas assignment was announced. When I heard the destination was England, I said to myself, "That's where I will go. I'll be on that ship, pleurisy or no pleurisy. I won't tell anybody I'm sick." And that's what I did.

Before we could leave for England, we had to go to Brooklyn to take a week or so of safety and orientation training— how to put on a gas mask and that sort of thing. We stayed in a black hotel, and I was assigned to supervise the black girls who were going over. There was one problem that I had to take care of immediately. I heard that a group of white girls had been scheduled for their training ahead of us, and we would have to wait until they were finished. I called a meeting of my group, told them the situation, and then said, "I have a plan. We'll all get up early tomorrow morning and be at the training area before the white girls arrive. Are you with me?" They said, "Yes, we are with you, Mrs. Street."

The next morning we were present and ready for training when the white girls got there. The Red Cross trainer came over to me and said, "You're not supposed to be here. You'll take your training later." I said, "Well, that's news to me. We are here and we are going to take our training now." So what could he do? He didn't like it, but he let us take our training with the white girls. I was surprised that he let me get away with it, but he did! We all finished the training course—black and white—at the same time.

Finally, the time came for us to board the *Queen Mary*. It was so exciting to be traveling on that ship. I had seen it once before when I was visiting New York, but I never dreamed that one day I'd be a passenger on my way to Red Cross service in

With other Red Cross workers just before boarding the
Queen Mary

England. I was put in charge of the seven black women. In
fact, I should have been in charge of all 121 Red Cross workers on their way to England because I had the highest title. I
was designated assistant club director with the equilvalent military rank of captain. They said that was in case I should be
captured, the enemy would know how to treat me. Nobody
else in the Red Cross group had a rank that high. But I was
passed over, and a white girl was put in charge of all of us.

There was never any friction between her and me. I didn't
allow it to develop. Of course, I already knew that in the real
world people don't always get what they deserve. I didn't get
the position because I was black, and I knew who was responsible. The man who had trained us in Brooklyn was responsible for me being slighted. I had a way of getting back at him.
When he came on board to say farewell to us, I told my girls
to shun him and not speak to him. If he could slight us, we
could slight him. And we did.

Furthermore, we had certain compensations. I saw to it that my seven girls and I were assigned to the most spacious and comfortable state rooms. We worked especially hard and always won the daily inspections and got to have dinner with the captain. The ship was loaded with thousands of soldiers, but we didn't see much of them. They were way down in the bowels of the ship crowded together, they said, like sardines. Compared to them, we had luxury quarters. We spent most of our time playing games and going to picture shows. We also spent a lot of time being seasick! Sooner or later, all of us got sick and vomited. It was hard for any of us to hold any food down during the week or more it took to go over, especially during the period when we almost got torpedoed. You see, the most exciting—and dangerous—incident of the trip was being chased by a German submarine for five days. During that episode our ship had to take a zig-zag course to outmaneuver it. Everybody really got sick then. Of course, we didn't notice that too much because we were afraid we'd be torpedoed and sunk any minute.

I knew that my brother Webster, who was in the Signal Corps, was going overseas about the same time I was. So I asked the captain of our ship if the 258th Signal Corps men were on board his ship. He said, "No, but that unit is in the convoy just ahead." From then on, I tried to hook up with him. When we got to Scotland, I made an attempt to locate him but was told he'd already been shipped to England. I tracked him all the way until I finally caught up with him. I was already at my station in Portsmouth, England, and was walking to the service club where I worked one day when I saw some young black soldiers working on some telephone poles. I asked them what outfit they were with, and they said it was the 258th Signal Corps. I said, "I have a brother named Webster Taylor with your outfit. Where are you stationed?" They said, "Oh, he's down at our camp."

So I called his commanding officer and said, "Do you have a young man by the name of Webster Demetrius Taylor in your outfit?" He said, "Yes, I do." I said, "Well, I'm his sister. I'm assistant club director with the American Red Cross up here in Southampton, and I'd like for you to let my brother come up to see me this weekend." He said, "Oh, I can do better than that. I'll bring him up." So he brought Webster up that Sunday afternoon. Then I said, "Captain, you have eighteen men detached for service here in Southampton. Can't you let my brother join these men while I'm here?" He said, "Of course, I can." Webster said, "Well, I'd like to be close to you, Mae, but I hate to leave my friends." The captain said, "Aw come on Taylor, your sister is here. Don't you want to be near her? I'll have your things sent." And he did. I got to see my brother about every other day for about six weeks while he was on duty there.

Let me back up now and tell you how I was responsible for the formation of the 258th Signal Corps. It came about this way. My brother was a student at Louisville Municipal College, the black division of the University of Louisville, when he dropped out to join the Signal Corps. He and seventeen other young black men went to Lexington for their training, and when he finished the course, he called me one night almost in tears. "Sister," he said, "I came here to be in the Signal Corps, but now they're sending us all to the infantry. I don't want to be in the infantry." I said, "Don't worry about it, Webster. I'll see what I can do."

The next day I got in my car, stopped by Lincoln Institute and picked up Mr. Whitney Young Sr. for company, and by eight o'clock I was at the gate of the Signal Corps camp. When I found the commander of the camp, I said, "My brother came here to train to be in the Signal Corps, and now he's being put in the infantry. Will you please do something?" He said, "I'll attend to that, Mrs. Street." The next week Webster was sent to a Signal Corps unit in Missouri. I said nothing about his color, and the officer evidently assumed my brother was white because he thought I was. On his transfer papers he put down white as his color. Webster was a light brown, and it

With other Red Cross workers and black soldiers in
Southampton, England

wasn't until he arrived at the camp in Missouri that they realized the mistake. The army brass was in a dilemma! These
were the days before the armed services were integrated, and
they solved the problem by organizing the 258th Signal Corps
for blacks. Webster was trained in Missouri, then sent to Alaska
before he was shipped to England. Having him close by for
those few weeks helped me get used to being overseas.

Before I was finally assigned to my permanent duty station in Portsmouth, I had been through Bourse, Scotland, and
sent by train down to London for three weeks of orientation.
The first food I ate on European soil was some cold lamb sand-
wiches on that train. It was awful! I would have given anything for some good Kentucky cooking. I was in a bad mood
and when we arrived in London things got worse. I couldn't
find my luggage. I asked a Red Cross official where it was, and
she said, "It's across the street where it belongs." I said, "What
do you mean, 'where it belongs'? It belongs here." She said,
"The black girls are housed in the left wing of this building on

the third floor. You will be in the building across the street." I said, "I'm sorry, sweetheart, but I'm one of those black girls. So please have my luggage brought over." The English woman didn't believe me and called the American director and said, "We've got a woman here named Mrs. Street, and she's got some kind of chip on her shoulder and wants her luggage moved to be with the black workers. What should I do?" He asked to speak to me and said, "Are you Mae Street?" I said, "Yes, I am." He said, "Honey, take the underground and bring all your girls on down here to the Red Cross office. I want to see you. You've got so much spunk you're already raising hell before you get settled down." When we got there, he said, "You make me happy to know you. We need more people like you. With women like you supporting our servicemen, we're gonna win this war."

I was made assistant director of a Red Cross service club for black soldiers in Southampton. That's where we fed and entertained soldiers who were waiting to be shipped across the English Channel to the war front. Our club was in a converted church building. We didn't have sleeping facilities, but we tried to make things pleasant for the frightened, nervous soldiers who came to the club. They knew that many of them were just a few hours away from the fighting and that some of them would never make it home. We tried to take their minds off their worries with music, games, and good food. My soldiers came from all over the United States, and I got to know quite a few from Louisville and Kentucky. Like me, a lot of them were trying to locate relatives that were also in the service. Of course, I met many individual soldiers who stand out in my memory. One of them was a fine pianist named Rudolph Dunbar, who later became the first black man to lead a German orchestra as conductor-in-chief of the Berlin Philharmonic. I got to know a young officer from Louisville named Rudy Winlock, whose sister was a good friend of mine. When he saw me at the club, he rushed over and hugged me like a long-lost friend. I also met my second husband, but I've already told you about that affair. Most of the soldiers were scared young men who were hoping and praying that they would survive the war and return home to their friends and loved ones.

The clientele for our club was all black because black and white soldiers were not allowed to mix in the armed services. The only racial incident I can remember happened one Sunday afternoon when I was in the club and overhead a white officer arguing with one of my black soldiers. I went over to the lieutenant and said, "What's wrong?" He said, "I'm telling this soldier how to wear his tie and uniform and how to behave properly." I said, "Sir, what right do you have coming into this club to chew out this young man? He looks all right to me, and his behavior is certainly better than yours. Is he in your command?" The officer said, "No, but I'm a first lieutenant and have rank over him." I said, "You have your own clubs and your own men to worry about. Would you mind leaving ours? You don't allow blacks in your club, so we don't want you in ours." He left.

Everything was in short supply, but I learned to scrounge for my soldiers. One time I was able to arrange for a fourteen-piece ensemble to play at the club on Sunday afternoons. It happened this way. A major called me one day a couple of weeks before Christmas and said, "Do you have any tinsel and balls and ornaments for a Christmas tree that you could share with us?" I said, "Yes, I think we do, but what can you share with us?" He said, "Well, I have a fourteen-piece band that you can have when we're not using it." I said all right and we did a swap. After our first dance, a soldier said, "Mrs. Street, you certainly keep this place jumping." And that's exactly what I wanted to do because it kept the soldiers' minds off the war that was waiting for them just a few miles away.

Indeed, World War II was an exciting period of our history, and as a Red Cross worker overseas I felt a part of that excitement. I felt that I was doing something good for my country. I loved to wear the Red Cross uniform and do my duty for the men who were doing their duty for all of us. I know I looked good in my uniform because people were often telling me so. When I left the Red Cross in 1945, I received a letter from the director of personnel services complimenting me on my administrative abilities, my initiative, my creativity, and my ability to work with people from many cultures and educational backgrounds. He even commented on my appearance: "Mrs. Street has a fine physique and personal appearance and inspires confidence and reflects enthusiasm." You can imagine how much I appreciated the good things he said about me in that letter.

Thirty-five years later I returned to Southampton and revisited the places I had known as a young woman during the war. Everything had changed so much and looked more like the United States. But I found the building where I had lived and the church where my service club was located. It had again been converted—this time back to a church. I also saw the hotel where I used to eat many of my meals. I didn't care much for English food then, and it hasn't improved very much over the years. But I did enjoy so much going back. It's a strange feeling to return to places where you lived so many years before. It's unreal. It's like being in a dream. You know that thirty or forty years before you sat at that desk or walked through that door, yet it seems hardly possible. You wonder, "Why am I here now? Was I ever really here all those many years ago?" I look around and I know that I was truly in that room. I know that over there in that corner was our Christmas tree where we sang carols and cried lonely tears. There under that stained glass window of Jesus the Good Shepherd was where our borrowed band played songs of love and separation. And here by that door is where I first saw James Meredith Kidd III. Yes, it was so very long ago, but it was all indeed real.

And yes, I remember well the voyage back home after I had finished my service in England. I remember that even as I took off my Red Cross uniform in Washington, D.C., I wasn't quite ready to return home and pick up the pieces of my life that I had left behind. Like a soldier suffering from battle fatigue, I needed a little more time to resume my civilian life. That's why I put in an application with the United Seamen's Service and soon moved to Portland, Maine, to live and work for a year. It turned out to be another fortunate career experience for me.

I found out after moving to Portland to work for United Seamen's Service that the young lady who had preceded me left because she said living in Portland wasn't like living in the United States—and it was too cold. Indeed, it was a long way from Kentucky and it was cold, but I didn't have any trouble at all. I can live anywhere so long as I like the work I do. I like any place I live if I like my work. And I liked what I was doing. Actually, it was somewhat like the work I did for the Red Cross in England.

When I returned to the States, therefore, I discovered that I wasn't ready to settle down back in Kentucky. I've heard soldiers say there are two kinds of soldiers—those who can't wait to get out of their uniforms and those who want to stay in them. I liked my Red Cross uniform and I wanted to stay in it. I looked good in it. People often complimented me on how good I looked. The war had ended, however, and there was no need any longer for my services with the Red Cross, so I looked around and discovered the United Seamen's Service, a chain of service clubs for merchant seamen. They were scattered all over the country in port cities like New York, Charleston, and San Diego and were designed to give merchant sailors places to go for food and shelter and entertainment while they were in port for a few days. I applied for a position with the United Seamen's Service and was appointed to Portland. I didn't go up there intending to stay there the rest of my life. I knew, however, that I needed a transitional job between my service during the war and my peacetime job in Louisville. I knew that in about a year I would be ready to go home. If I needed any further convincing, the coming of winter made me realize that I didn't want to live the rest of my life in such a cold climate. Heavy coats and boots were our main uniform for

With volunteers for the United Seamen's Service club in
Portland, Maine

The exterior of the United Seamen's
Service club in Portland

much of the time, and that wasn't quite the kind of uniform I had in mind.

Nevertheless, I liked Portland and I found a great deal of satisfaction in the work I did. The club was already successful when I arrived, but I soon realized that much more could be done to accommodate the sailors. I wanted to make our facilities in the Hotel Mariner a real home away from home for them. I decided to make our club more like the Hollywood Canteen, where movie stars met the soldiers and served as hostesses feeding and dancing and talking with them.

I met with the board of directors to ask for their support. I said, "This is a large port, and you do a lot of business with ships from all over the world. The men that work on those ships are important to you, and when they arrive in Portland, they need to have a decent place to relax and enjoy themselves. That's what we try to provide at United Seamen's Service. Now I know that you're afraid if your wives and daughters come to the club, something might happen to them; but it won't if you provide a good program and entertainment. We will keep the sailors busy when they come to port so they can't get into trouble, and we will entertain them so they will want to come back. It is better to have the men see decent women in this setting than indecent women on the streets. They take rooms in our hotel and eat food in our dining room. It is a clean, orderly place for them to stay. What I want are women of high character to act as hostesses when the men are in town. They can serve refreshments and act as hostesses when we have dances." By the time I finished my presentation, I had them convinced that my program was their program. They voted to support it, and we went ahead to develop a very successful program—one that was copied all over the country. In fact, I got a citation from the national office in New York, and we became a model club.

First, I began to enlist volunteers by going to one of the big downtown department stores and handing out brochures and talking with women about volunteering to work at the

A dance at the United Seamen's Service club in Portland

At a local reception in Portland

club. Eventually we had almost one hundred young women who worked as volunteers to entertain the seamen. I also went on the radio to build community support for wholesome programs for the sailors, and I succeeded in making Portland one of the most hospitable cities for merchant ships.

There were very few blacks in Portland. I remember very vividly one morning after I had been in town for several months that I was in my office and looked out the window and I saw a little black boy. He was the first black person I had seen in Portland. I don't know whether people in Portland knew I was black. I didn't tell them and they didn't ask me. All I know is that I was able to build on some of the organizational skills I had learned in my Red Cross work and develop my abilities in public relations. All of this experience was useful when I returned to my job at Mammoth and organized their first public relations program. I was building my career, step by step. It was like something was guiding me and pointing me in the direction I should go.

My Life in Politics

For seventeen years—from 1968 to 1985—I was called the "Lady of the House." Those were the years I served in the Kentucky General Assembly in Frankfort as representative from Louisville's Forty-first Legislative District. I was a member of a double minority. I was a black and a woman back when there were very few of us in elective offices. Like most blacks, I was a Democrat and voted in every election; but I had never been interested in politics. Never. I had run a successful campaign in Detroit some years before for a candidate for the city board of aldermen, but I was a paid worker. It was just a job. I was so apolitical I had never even been a precinct worker. My parents in Millersburg were voters, but they were never politically active. When I was a girl, they voted Republican. They were still voting for the party that had freed them, they said, and had not noticed that that party had changed since Lincoln's time. It was President Roosevelt's liberal social programs of the 1930s that made us blacks into Democrats.

My only personal political involvement had been two years before my election, when I helped a friend lose her race for Louisville alderman. She asked me to work inside the polling place as her observer, but I told her I would work outside. I said, "It's too stuffy sitting in there all day, but I will hand out flyers and campaign for you on the street." I also had a neighborhood picnic for her in my back yard with hot dogs, potato chips, and soft drinks. I didn't seem to do her any good because she lost the election by a wide margin.

I had good qualifications, however, to be a viable candidate for my own election. I was active in church and commu-

107

nity organizations. I was a successful businesswoman. I was a poised speaker who looked good in public. And I had opinions on issues that affect people. So I guess it was natural for me to go into politics when I was approached by the Democratic party to run for a legislative seat held for a long time by the Republicans. My name was suggested to the Democratic Executive Committee as a person who could win the election, and J. B. Smith, an insurance executive, and Mrs. Maude Benbow, whose husband was a prominent bondsman, were given the job of convincing me to run. When they came to see me, I said, "I appreciate the honor of being asked, but I do not like politics." They kept on talking about what an ideal candidate I would make and that I was the only hope the Democrats had to unseat the Republican representative. I said, "I cannot tell you yes because I do not like politics." Still, they wouldn't take no for an answer and left reminding me how well-known and respected I was. As they left, I said, "I'm sorry you've wasted your time, but my answer is still no."

Two weeks later Mr. Smith called me again. I said, "You do not hear very well, do you? I said I'm not interested in getting into politics. The answer is no." A few days later, he called again. Even though he was a good friend, I was getting exasperated with his persistence. I said, "You again? You just won't take no for an answer." He said, "That's right. We need you. This time I hope you will say yes." My husband was in the room and heard me talking and said, "Go ahead, Mae, and say yes, and I will help you. You're tired of your insurance work. They don't treat you fairly. This may be a change you will like. Go for it." Finally, I agreed, and said, "All right, I'll give it a try. Now you need to know that when I start something, I intend to do it right. I expect to win. I will work hard and I expect everybody else to also."

Indeed, I cannot complain about the support I received. I had some token opposition in the Democratic primary, but I won easily. Then the Democratic party supported me financially, and the labor unions got behind me. Mr. Kidd, who

At her seat in the Kentucky General Assembly

was teaching science at Shawnee Junior High, was a great help
to me in organizing my campaign and developing strategy. He
and I sat at this kitchen table and worked out a plan for victory. First, I based my platform on the promise that I would
always tell the truth to the voters. Then I began canvassing
the legislative district in order to meet the voters. I wanted to
involve as many people in my campaign as I could—from the
very young to the very old. Even the children who were too
young to vote were important to me. I told the voters that I
would be representing everyone in my district in Frankfort,
regardless of age or sex or color or anything else. In fact, the
children helped to get me elected. With the permission of their
parents, I organized a kind of children's brigade to help me
distribute campaign flyers every afternoon from five to eight.

They had to be nine or ten years old and they had to be clean and neatly dressed. I'd pick up a carload of children and take them to a different neighborhood each evening, where we'd knock on doors, meet the people, and distribute the fly-ers. It was in the fall of the year and most people were on their porches or sitting in their yards, and it was easy to talk to them.

The children were better campaigners than I was. One day I picked them up as usual, but I was already tired from other duties, and I said, "I'm just too tired to go out this evening. Let's call it off." One of the boys said, "Aw, Mrs. Kidd, you promised that we would do such-and-such a street today. Aw, come on. Let's do it." What could I do? I agreed. In fact, their youth and energy boosted me when I was exhausted. They liked riding in my car and meeting people and being part of an important project. They liked me because I treated them with respect. Every evening after we finished our rounds I'd take them by my house and give them soft drinks and cookies, and on Saturday I gave them a little spending change. They played a vital role in my election victory.

Indeed, I won—by more than a two-to-one majority. My Republican opponent was a black man who lived down the street from me and worked in the post office. He was from a lovely family, but I simply out-campaigned him. After his de-feat he said, "There was no way I could win. I couldn't beat that woman. I couldn't beat those children she had working for her. Everywhere I'd go, she'd already been, and people would say, 'Oh, I'm sorry but I promised Mrs. Kidd I'd vote for her.' She just worked too hard for me." Of course, I was very proud that I had won. Not only would I be able to do some good things for my constituents, but I would be able to hold my head up high when I saw the people from Mammoth who had mistreated me. They looked like fools when I was elected. They took on and said how proud they were, but I knew they were just trying to play up to me.

That race was the first of eight that I won. I was popular in my district because I maintained good relations with my constituents. I didn't forget them between elections. I kept in close touch with people and organizations throughout my district, from the Russell Area Council and the Plymouth Settlement House to the Portland Community Council. Most of the people in Portland are white, and they became very dear to me. My home was my office, and people knew they could call me or come by to see me anytime. I had my side porch glassed in for my office, and I had a phone, a desk, and my files in it. People knew they could call on me when they had a problem because I knew how to get things done. They still call on me, and I've been out of office for almost ten years.

I ran nine times and was elected eight times. I never even came close to being defeated, but I never took it for granted that I would win. People would say, "Mae, why are you running so hard? Everybody knows you are going to win." I would say, "I would like to win, but I won't if you don't vote for me." I ran every other year from 1968 until 1984, the year I lost to the present incumbent, Mr. Tom Riner. I had some opposition in the Democratic primary, but I always won. The Republicans began puting up a white opponent in the general election, and I whipped them all until Mr. Riner came along and spent a lot of money to oppose me. You could say he bought the election.

I suppose I could still be in office if I had been willing to compromise my principles. I said, "I will never pay anyone, directly or indirectly, to vote for me. If they don't trust me and believe in what I've done for them, then I'll lose." And so I did. But I went down to defeat with my head high. I have heard that Mr. Riner spent around $47,000 getting elected over me. He is a white man who calls himself a preacher. My old district has been gerrymandered out into the East End and is now predominantly white. When I was first elected, it was mainly black, with some scattered pockets of whites in neighborhoods like Portland. Even the whites liked me because they voted for me and I carried their neighborhoods. I hope the voters are pleased with the man who replaced me, although I don't see any good he's done.

But that's water over the dam. And maybe it was time for me to retire anyway. After all, I was eighty years old, and during my seventeen years in politics I had accomplished quite a lot. Let me tell you about some of the highlights of my political career. First of all, on my first day you'd better believe I was so happy and proud to be going to Frankfort to become a legislator. In those days blacks couldn't stay in good motels or hotels, so I arranged to stay with the Robb family when the legislature was in session. That morning I drove by the Robbs, left my bags, and rushed over to the House chamber. I found my desk, sat down, and felt like a complete stranger. I didn't know anybody. I didn't recognize a soul. I knew several of the Jefferson County representatives by name, but I wouldn't have recognized them. At the same time, I was so excited I felt like I was walking on air.

I got so many flowers on my first day that my desk and the aisles were covered. "Please get rid of your flowers," the men around me asked good-naturedly. "We can't even move." So I got someone to help me take the flowers to my car, and I took them to the Robbs. But the next day I was again swamped with flowers and cards, and I had to take them out again. All those flowers made me feel so good. All the other legislators got to know who I was because I was the lady who got all the flowers. They also got to know me because I like hats and I wore one each day to my desk. Several of the men complained— again in a good-natured way—that they couldn't see the speaker's platform because of my hats, so I stopped wearing them, except on special occasions. One way or another, people began to notice me, even before I started introducing bills. Of course, I also began to introduce myself to people and soon knew everybody.

My first year I made a good record for myself. First, I got to know the man who was in charge of writing bills in the correct form that we would submit for debate and vote. Then,

I was always talking with people in order to make friends. I was polite and courteous, and I tended to my own business. I didn't have any special friends in the legislature, but I tried to be friendly with everyone. I did, however, become a friend of Georgia Davis, the black woman from Louisville who was elected to the Senate the year I was elected to the House. Kentucky has never elected many blacks to public office, but we were not the first ones to go to Frankfort. There had been a few other blacks to serve in the Kentucky General Assembly. In fact, Charles W. Anderson Jr. was a black Louisville lawyer who was elected as a Republican House member in 1935.

I decided that since so many of the people in my district were low-income families, I would focus my energies on housing — open housing and low-cost housing. The open-housing bill was introduced in the state Senate by Senator Georgia Davis and in the House by Hughes McGill. After a lengthy and sometimes bitter debate, it passed in the Senate by 27 to 3. In the House it passed by 54 to 17. I worked day and night to get the bill approved. When the bill passed, we cried tears of joy. It was a milestone in Kentucky history.

The open-housing bill simply provided that anyone could live anywhere he had the money to pay for it. Specifically, the bill prohibits discrimination by reason of race, color, religion, or national origin in the sale or rental of housing and gave the Human Rights Commission the power to enforce the law. Louisville already had an open-housing ordinance, but this bill took precedence and covered the entire state. It meant that whether you lived in Pikeville or Paducah, you could live where you wanted to — if you could afford to. Of course, that was the catch. The white man always has had the advantage over us blacks because he has the money. If you don't have money, you can't do certain things the law allows. You can't live in good housing. You can't have decent food and clothing. Segregation by economics is still with us, but at least now the law is on the side of equal justice. Even the Republican governor, Louie B. Nunn, saw the handwriting on the wall.

He had been an enemy of open housing legislation in his campaign and maintained that anyone has the right to sell or refuse
to sell his house to anyone for any reason. It was a major surprise of the 1968 session of the General Assembly when, on
March 27, he allowed the open-housing bill to become law
without his signature.

During my freshman year, I was learning the ropes and
becoming recognized as someone to be taken seriously. Bill
Powell, a political writer for the *Courier-Journal*, took notice
of me and selected me to write about in his column. There is
a clipping from the *Courier-Journal*, dated March 20, 1968, in
which Mr. Powell calls the bill "a step towards ending discrimination against Negroes" and said that Kentucky was "the first
in all the South to adopt an open housing law of any kind."
About me, he wrote: "She has won many awards and has spent
a lifetime quietly—without apparent militance—trying to give
the Negro a break." This is the way he described me after the
bill was passed in the House: "Mrs. Mae Street Kidd stood to
thank the House members for the vote. She was unable to say
anything for a long time. She just stood there with her eyes
fixed on the microphone she held in her hands. Finally she
spoke in a few eloquent words and then in spite of all she could
do the tears started." Mr. Powell pointed out that this bill was
passed when there were only three black members in the entire legislature: Georgia Davis, Hughes McGill, and Mae Street
Kidd.

Throughout my legislative career, I never considered myself a representative who did special favors for black people. I
didn't consider myself their representative. Everything I did
was for the good of all people—black, green, gray, or white. I
didn't go to Frankfort hollering, "Do this for me because I'm
black." I never used race as a justification for any bill or project
I supported. I was in Frankfort for all the people of my district
and for all the people of Kentucky. I wanted to help all the
people, and I did. I wish I could be put down in history as a

A flyer for Mae Street Kidd's 1970 re-election campaign

representative who tried to help more people than anybody before me.

If I felt a special obligation to anyone, however, it was to the low-income people of all races and colors. Mr. Powell wrote in this article on March 11, 1970: "She is not just a Negro woman fighting for a cause; she is well-rounded in her attention to bills for all the public." He added that I had "extremely broad interests and extremely broad effectiveness." A few years

With (l. to r.) Julian Carroll, Georgia Davis Powers,
Norbert Blume, Charlotte Smith, and Wendell Ford

later Governor Ford called me "a worker for people"—and he
didn't say white people or black people—just people.

During my freshman term, I was selected for a unique
honor—to escort the governor to the house chamber. Another
honor was to be assigned to the Rules Committee, the first
woman to be chosen. When my birthday rolled around on
February 8, you would have thought I was president of the
United States because I received a cake and many bouquets
of flowers. As time went on, I became the first woman to be
selected as secretary of the Democratic Caucus. I was also
elected chairman of the Enrollment Committee, which re-
ceives and handles bills from the Senate.

I was also learning how to be a politician. For example, I
learned that a legislator never tells his colleagues about the
bills he plans to write and introduce. You don't tell anybody
what you're planning to do, or they will jump ahead and steal
it from you. You learn to keep your mouth shut. You just go
ahead and do it. It's a secret that you keep until you introduce
the bill. As I was getting more experience, I was moving on

up. I mean that literally. When I was a freshman, I had to sit near the back of the House chamber. When I began to get some seniority, I was able to move up closer to the speaker's desk. By 1970 I was seated in the third row between a Mr. Huff of Laurel County and Mr. Wilson Wyatt Jr. of Jefferson County.

Another bill that I promoted was House Bill 137, which provided for a statewide program for the prevention, screening, diagnosis, and treatment of lead poisoning, which was passed at the following legislative session and signed into law by our new governor, a Democrat, Wendell Ford. I got interested in this issue because so many of the families in my district live in old houses with leaded paint pealing off the walls and floors. Children were putting the poisonous paint in their mouths and getting sick.

My big project during the 1970 legislative session, however, was a bill to create a Kentucky housing corporation to provide mortgage loans for low-income people. When I introduced the bill, Governor Nunn was against it. But I was able to convince enough legislators to support it and it passed. It's not easy to get a bill passed, especially a controversial one that plows new ground. You've got to convince a lot of people to vote for it. Some of the legislators said, "If we don't vote for her bill, Mrs. Kidd will choke us with our neckties." I didn't exactly say that, but I didn't care what they said I said as long as they voted for the bill. The bill passed but Governor Nunn vetoed it. I tried to rewrite the bill to eliminate his objections and introduced and passed a second bill. Guess what? He also vetoed it. I was ready to give up on him—but not on the bill.

At the next session in 1972, we had a new governor and I was ready to try again. Before the session began, I read in the paper that one of the committees was previewing my bill, so I got in my car and went to the room where they were meeting in Frankfort and said, "Good morning, gentlemen." They said, "Good morning, Mae. What can we do for you?" I said, "I'm glad that you are going to review my bill, and I'm here to sup-

In committee

With a colleague in the General Assembly

port it. I want you to know that it is my bill, so do not mess with it." I knew there were still a few legislators who didn't take me seriously. I wanted them to know I meant business. They laughed and I said, "Now if you can do anything to improve it, I will be grateful, but don't ruin it. And don't take my bill away from me. It is my bill." They knew I meant it. They made a few suggestions, but they did support it.

It was a controversial bill, and I knew I had to have 51 votes to pass it. One of the most vocal opponents was a clothing store owner from the mountains named Dawahare. He got up eight or nine times to attack the bill, and finally the Speaker of the House said, "Mr. Dawahare, you cannot speak again. You have used up all your time. We know where you stand." After one of his attacks on the bill, I got up and said, "I feel sorry for this gentlemen. What would he do if early one morning he was shaving and looking at himself in the mirror and suddenly, before his own eyes, he turned black? Would he cut his throat or just jump in the river? I feel sorry for the gentleman that he should live in such fear of black people." I was very nervous as we approached the final vote on the bill. I had told the Speaker that I wanted him to lock the voting machine as soon as I got 51 votes so that nobody could change his vote. It was finally passed by both houses and in 1972 Governor Ford signed it. In 1974 I introduced a bill to make the Kentucky Housing Corporation more flexible, and we passed it too.

In all, I served under five Kentucky governors—Louie Nunn, Julian Carroll, Wendell Ford, John Y. Brown, Jr., and Martha Layne Collins. I knew them all well enough to talk with them personally in their office. I knew them and they knew me. A good representative has to get to know the governor. You can't be a stranger to the governor and be a good representative of your district. I got along with all five of them. I wasn't silly enough to get into an argument with Governor Nunn, even when he opposed my low-cost housing bill. I just ignored him when he disagreed with me.

With Edward Kennedy and Rep. Carl Hines

Julian Carroll was the governor who was most coopera-
tive with me. He was the last governor to have a contingency
fund that he could use at his discretion for special projects. I
was one of the few legislators who used that opportunity to get
money to help their home districts. I got $35,000 for an Ur-
ban League project, $33,000 for the Lincoln Foundation to
restore Whitney M. Young Sr.'s birthplace, $7,500 for the
YMCA—in all, over $100,000 for Louisville projects. Gover-
nor Carroll told his top man, Dr. Jack Hall, to listen to me
whenever I wanted money and let me have it if it was a good
cause. I preferred to work with Dr. Hall anyway. He was more
on my level and had more time for me. He was on loan to the
governor from the University of Kentucky, and he was never
too busy to talk to me. On the other hand, when you go to see
a governor, before you get seated comfortably, he's likely to
stand up on you and say, "Well Mae, I have to go to a meeting." I never did like for anybody to stand up on me for any
reason, governor or no governor!

So I made friends with Dr. Hall and he heard my requests for money. When I went to see him about a project, I took an easel and charts to show him what we would do with it. I said, "Dr. Hall, you just sit there and listen to me. I'll prove to you that we need this money, and I'll show you how we'll spend it." For example, I had charts to show how we'd renovate and decorate the Whitney Young house. Dr. Hall would sit there and listen and smile and then take his recommendation to the governor, who always approved it. The reason I never asked Dr. Hall for anything I didn't get is that we're both good salesmen. I presented a good case to him, and he then presented it to the governor. I also contacted state agencies when necessary to help my district. One time I got the highway department to repair the pedestrian walkway across the Riverside Expressway, and I also worked for a bill that enabled Kentucky to take advantage of federal aid for the Meals on Wheels program. That benefited a lot of people in my district.

As I said earlier, during my first year in the General Assembly, I stayed with a family named Robb. They were in the undertaking business. If I had commuted each day from Louisville to Frankfort, it would have been fifty miles each way, and that's a lot of miles. The Robbs invited me to stay with them and didn't charge me anything, but each month I always gave them something for my room and dinner. Sometimes I'd buy some Cornish hens—maybe ten at a time—and leave them in their refrigerator. Sometimes I would leave them some money. They were rich and didn't need anything from me, but Mae Street Kidd won't stay on anybody for nothing! They were good to me, and I was so grateful to them. To this day, their granddaughter calls me Aunt Mae. They had a son named Jackson Robb, who was a beautiful pianist and organist. He could play both at the same time. Sometimes he'd be playing at two o'clock in the morning, and the neighbors would call on the phone to say how much they were enjoying his music.

I stayed with the Robbs because it was hard for blacks to

With then–Speaker of the House Julian Carroll

With then-governor Wendell Ford

Presenting Governor Julian
Carroll with a plaque

At Governor's Mansion reception with Governor
John Y. Brown Jr

find a decent motel or hotel that would take them. By the time
I left office, I could have stayed at any place I wanted to. That's
how much things had changed in seventeen years. In those
days there weren't many nice places for anybody to stay, white
or black. Now there are beautiful places. One of the best is
the Capital Plaza Hotel, which was built by Governor Wallace
Wilkinson. A few years ago when I went over there to speak at
a Martin Luther King Day celebration, I complimented Mr.
Wilkinson for thinking enough of our capital city to build us
a decent hotel. He was sitting at the head table, and when he
spoke, he said, "Mrs. Kidd, do you mind if I come down and
hug you?"

During my years in the legislature I was involved in a lot
of legislation. I sponsored a bill to give a temporary increase
in the occupational tax for the public schools in Louisville
and Jefferson County during the time of their merger. I used
my influence to help make Martin Luther King's birthday a
state holiday. In 1974 I opposed the reinstatement of the death
penalty in Kentucky because it falls heaviest on the poor and
the black. Anyway, I believe that life imprisonment is a worse
punishment than death. Put a criminal in prison for life—and
don't pamper him too much—and he'll wish he had died! I
also fought against the bill requesting an antibusing amend-
ment to the United States Constitution. I said it would turn
back the clock and undo some of the progress we had made
in race relations, but it passed in the house by 84 to 8. Oh yes,
the death penalty was reinstated too. Well, you don't win every time.

One of my proudest achievements was the ratification of
the Thirteenth, Fourteenth, and Fifteenth amendments to the
U.S. Constitution in 1976. Believe it or not, but Kentucky had
never officially passed the amendments abolishing slavery and
granting the freed slaves the right to vote and full citizenship.
This is how that happened. One day my assistant, a lady named
Miller, came to me and said, "Mrs. Kidd, I've just found out
that these amendments have never been ratified by Kentucky."

I couldn't believe it! I hit the ceiling! For 112 years Kentucky had not acted on those amendments, even though they had become law without Kentucky's support. I thought it was high time we caught up with the rest of the country. It was obvious to me that no white person was ever going to get them passed. For over a century they had said no. All those years I felt that Kentucky had been saying: "You black people are still slaves, and that's the way you should remain." So I knew it was up to a black person to get the job done. I said to Mrs. Miller, "Well, we'll just have to do something about that." So we finished up the project we were working on and got busy with the amendments resolution.

Mrs. Miller came back a few days later with the resolution written according to the legal requirements. When it passed unanimously, I think everyone was pleased. It was especially important to me because I am a proud Kentuckian, and I didn't want that blot to remain on our history. I felt that the ratification was good for all Kentuckians because it lifted an embarrassing burden from the shoulders of both blacks and whites. Sometimes I would have a co-sponsor for a bill, but I didn't want one for this resolution. Senator Powers introduced it in the Senate and got it passed there. Oddly enough, there was no celebration when the resolution was adopted, but a lot of people sent me congratulations. I felt that with the ratification of those amendments we had at last ended the Civil War in Kentucky.

Esquire Magazine chose me to receive their 1976 Achievement Award, and in 1985 Governor Martha Layne Collins sent me to Philadelphia to represent her and the Commonwealth of Kentucky at the celebration of National Freedom Day. It was one of the proudest moments of my life. For a while my husband was a little jealous of my achievements and the attention that people paid me, but eventually even he was proud of me.

Yes, I think I have been amply rewarded for my service in the General Assembly. It was a capstone to my career. When I left Millersburg at the age of twenty-one, I never dreamed that one day I would have a desk in the Kentucky state capitol. I am so pleased that my mother lived to see it. She told me that a lot of whites in Millersburg told her, "We are so proud of your daughter." I said, "That was kind of them to say so, but had I stayed in Millersburg and run for office, I would never have made it to Frankfort." The people in Millersburg were — and are — too busy living the good life to be very progressive. Meanwhile, I've been living the rugged life of achievment. Well, come to think of it, I've lived the good life too.

Lives of Service

The Bible says, "By your fruits shall ye be known." In other words we will be judged not by what we say, not by how much noise we make, not by our public acclaim, not by our position, not by our income, not by our skin color. We are all judged by what we produce. The fruits of our labors tell us what kind of life we have lived. Of course, the Bible also says, "Judge not that ye be judged." In other words, be careful how you estimate a person's worth—your own or anybody else's. It is only the eye of God that sees how worthy we really are.

Despite these cautions, we are constantly appraising, judging, critiquing everything and everyone from the head of lettuce in the supermarket to the head of the local school board. It is part of our nature, and I make no apology for my own assessments of myself and my friends. I will try to be honest and open and fair—well, as much as I can be. So now it is time for me to talk about lives of service—my own and those of people I have known. I call them all friends, even though I've known some of them very little. Each one has lived a life of service in a unique way and has made a positive impact on my own life.

I don't mean to sound defensive or immodest, but I want to begin by saying some things about my service to others, especially my contributions to my own race. Some people have been critical of me, and I want to put my contributions to civil rights on record. During my lifetime I have seen tremendous advances in opportunities for African Americans in this country. As we know, the people in power do not easily and readily give it up to newcomers. White males have been in charge of

our country for all of our history. The advances made by
women, blacks, and other minorities have been forced upon
the white men in control of our government, our economy,
our cultural life—everything. Women and blacks have led the
way in demanding full equality. How have they led this cru-
sade? Each person is different and each person works out his
life and destiny in a different way. Some people express themselves by confrontation. They thrive on butting heads with the
opposition. They lead demonstrations in the streets, at the
lunch counters, at the schoolhouse door, at the personnel office.

Other people take a quieter, more subtle route. This is
my way. I do not like violence. I do not like to bump up against
people and push them around or allow them to push me
around. I don't even like ugliness and violence on the television screen. When Alex Haley's *Roots* was on television, I
watched it until I began seeing white men whipping black men
and black men whipping each other. In my own life, I have
tried to avoid violence while standing up for what I believe in.
I never led a demonstration or a sit-in or pushed my way into
a whites-only seat. That was not my way. Yet I believe I have
done my share of civil rights work that has benefited everyone.

It should be apparent if you've listened to me thus far that
I am not one to be shoved around. I stand up for what is right.
In my articles, in my speeches, in my business and professional
work, in my political career—in all my activities I have been a
supporter of equal rights for all. My civil rights work has taken
the form of words. I have spoken in schools, churches, and
clubs trying to get people to register to vote. I pushed for equal
rights in the Kentucky General Assembly. As a businesswoman
I expected fair treatment and said so, even though I didn't usually receive it. But perhaps my most important service to my
sex and to my race is my life, which I have tried to live as an
example of what a black person could achieve—not just any

With schoolchildren

black person—but a black woman from a modest background who had to pull herself up.

Let me give you a few examples of how I refused to accept second-class citizenship. I don't intentionally put myself in a position where someone can insult me. On the other hand, I'm not going to be subservient to anyone. If I have to set you straight, I'll do it in a rational, intelligent way. I don't go around ranting and raving. Before my brother Webster Taylor and I went overseas during World War II—he was with a black Signal Corps unit and I was with the American Red Cross—we decided to visit our mother in Kentucky. He met me in Washington, where I was preparing for my work overseas, and we boarded a train. Webster and I were comfortably seated in a Jim Crow car as was the custom. Webster was dark brown and I was light enough to pass for white. Soon after the train pulled out of the station, the conductor came up to me and said,

"Young lady, you'll have to move to another coach." I looked at him, said nothing, and resumed talking with my brother.

About an hour later, while we were passing through Virginia, the conductor came back and said, "Lady, I'm sorry to have to disturb you, but you're going to have to move to another coach." I looked him squarely in the eye and said, "Please leave me alone. I'm comfortable where I am." I knew, of course, that he assumed I was white and had gotten on the black coach by mistake. I didn't budge from my seat. I didn't offer him an explanation. He must have given up because he never bothered me again, and I rode with my brother until our trip ended in Millersburg. That's the way I took my stand.

Although I never considered myself an advocate for black people exclusively in public or professional or private life, I have been active in many projects that benefited people of my race. In Louisville, for example, I helped raise money for the black YMCA, the black Girl Scouts, and the Lincoln Foundation. I have been active in the Phillis Wheatley branch of the YWCA and a member of the League of Women Voters. In 1948 I organized the first Urban League Guild outside of New York City. We were a kind of public relations department for that civil rights organization. Guild members helped to identify the needs of the community; then we pushed and promoted the Urban League and raised money for the projects. I was an important black official in the 1983 gubernatorial campaign of Dr. Harvey Sloane, when I was named state co-chairman.

One summer in the 1980s, when I was still in the Kentucky legislature, I helped save the J. O. Blanton House when HUD was about to take it back from the private corporation that was running it. The Blanton House is a high rise residence on Muhammad Ali Boulevard that serves mostly elderly black people. It required a residency rate of around 85 percent to break even, and it wasn't making it. HUD brought in a man named Higgins to manage the building. He came to me and asked if I would help him bring it up to standards, and I said I would.

On a business trip

I opened an office in the building and began to work twelve-hour days, sometimes even without taking a lunch break. I publicized the building and interviewed people to find out if they had a low enough income to qualify them to live there. The rent is subsidized by the government according to how much you can afford to pay. The larger your income the higher your rent. During that summer I raised the occupancy rate way above 85 percent and helped save the Blanton House from being taken over by HUD.

I've also helped individuals in quiet ways without any fanfare. Once I knew a woman who wanted to get into politics, but she was too timid to stand up and speak before a group. I talked with her, tried to reassure her and build up her pride, then went with her to a meeting where she got up and made a fine speech. It was the beginning of her journey of self-development. She now has a responsible job and is mayor of one of the small cities in Jefferson County.

When I was selling life insurance, I always tried to look
out for my clients. One day a man called me from the hospital. He said, "Mrs. Kidd, I'm very sick and not expected to live.
You sold me a $27,000 policy and my premium is due, and I
don't have the money to pay it. If I die I want to leave my
family a little money from my policy." I said, "Let me see what
I can do." I checked his records and found that he was paying
his premium annually, which meant that each payment was
fairly large. I changed the mode of payment to quarterly, which
made it possible for him to keep his insurance in force. He
lived for a few more months and died, but his insurance was
paid up and his family was protected.

The company had to pay out the value of the policy, but
the man's family deserved it. That's why people buy life insurance. He had held his policy for a long time. Of course, I could
have said, "Oh, I'm so sorry. There's nothing I can do for you.
You'll have to pay the total amount or your policy will lapse."
When I worked out the new payment plan, I didn't feel that I
was being disloyal to the company. In fact, it became a good
public relations story. The company asked me if I would
present the check for $27,000 to the widow, and I was pleased
to do it. I had made it possible for the widow and her children
to have some money to live on. Without my help, she would
have lost it all. Throughout my insurance career, I felt an obligation not only to the company but to my policyholders.
When I sell something to a person, I am on his side. I'm in his
corner.

I didn't have a lot of formal education. In fact, I didn't
even finish high school. But I've succeeded in several careers.
Most of them have been service careers in the public interest—my service in politics, in the insurance business, the
American Red Cross, and the United Seamen's Service. I have
worked all my life to serve people. I have served people in my
community, my state, and in my country. What more could I
have done? Many years ago I wrote a little poem I called "Life,"
in which I emphasized the importance of work. It begins: "Life

At the ceremony to transfer the Lincoln Institute's property

is more than drink and eat / And brave the long years through, / Since life is never quite complete, / Without some task to do." Indeed, it's an understatement to say that my work has been my life. And I hope it serves as an inspiration to young people today. I hope I can show them that the truly important things in life are achieved only through hard work.

Perhaps my life of work and service short-changed me in some areas. I was like a lot of young women today—except I was a couple of generations ahead of them. I wanted to have a career, and I waited until I was too old to have children. I confess that I never wanted children enthusiastically, but Mr. Street did. I even went to the doctor and took tests to see what could be done, but nothing could help me. Soon after it was determined that I couldn't have children, we brought my half-sister and half-brother, Mary Evelyn and Webster Taylor, to live with us and go to school. They became our subsitute children. Mary Evelyn was with us for seven years and finished elementary and high school in Louisville and went on to college at Virginia Union in Richmond, Virginia.

Webster was in and out of our home. He was at Lincoln

Institute, in the army, at Howard; and when he came home for the summer I'd get him a job with the Urban League. He wasn't a very good student because he was interested only in athletics. We took him out of Lincoln and sent him to St. Emma's Military School in Richmond, Virginia. It was a Catholic school and he did well there and made a good name for himself. One summer he helped remodel the Beecher Terrace housing project over on Walnut Street. After he served in the army he went to Howard University in Washington and studied engineering. I was very proud of both of them. Webster died a couple of years ago, but Mary Evelyn is still living in Paris, Kentucky.

Last Mother's Day at our church the minister asked all the mothers to stand. Then he asked for all the women who have helped raise other people's children to stand. I didn't stand. When church was out, one of the members who doesn't usually compliment anybody for anything rushed over to me and said, "Mae, why didn't you stand? Look at all the good things you've done for the children in your family and in other families. You've helped so many young people. You deserved to be recognized." I was pleased that she thought so.

I also think that if I hadn't been so busy with my careers I would have had more time for pastimes and hobbies. I do like to garden and have spent a lot of time in my yard, especially among my roses. For many years I have taken fresh roses to nearby nursing homes. I also like to write and read poetry. In school I loved Longfellow's poetry very much and still know by heart "The Wreck of the Hesperus" and "The Psalm of Life." I would recite those poems with gestures and great emotion in school. I also loved the poetry of Whittier and our black poets—especially Paul Laurence Dunbar, Countee Cullen, and Langston Hughes. We had two very good black poets here in Louisville, a father and son, Joseph Cotter Sr. and Joseph Cotter Jr. The young Cotter died before I came to Louisville, but I knew his father very well. Of the recent black poets, Maya

Angelou is my favorite. I loved the poem she recited at President Clinton's inauguration.

When I was a girl in Millersburg, I had a pony and cart and drove it around town. Sometimes I'd go out to my great-uncle's farm and my brother would put me in the saddle behind him and we'd gallop on down the pike. I'd be holding on to him scared to death I'd fall off. He'd say, "Don't worry, Mae. Just hold on. Hold on." I don't care much for horse racing, but I do like to go to the Kentucky Derby because it's such a dress-up occasion.

I've also found time in my busy life for various clubs and sororities and for an occasional trip. I love to fly. I've been flying since the 1940s. When I was public relations director for the National Negro Insurance Association, I flew to most of the major cities in the United States. A few years ago, I flew with my friend Clarice Tyree to Europe. We visited England and seven other European countries. Most of my earlier travel was business-connected. Mr. Street and Mr. Kidd and I very seldom took vacation trips. We were too busy working. This time I was traveling for enjoyment. We toured churches, art museums, historical sites—all the usual places tourists see— and we immersed ourselves in the different cultures. When we got home, we were thoroughly exhausted but happy with all the things we'd seen and done. I felt it was a vacation trip I deserved after a lifetime of hard work.

I think perhaps my most important influence has been as a role model for young women. I came along when both black and white women were dependent on males—first their fathers, then their husbands. I have showed them by my example that they can get along by themselves. They can be independent. They can be go-getters, achievers. Like me, if they see something they want, they can go get it. I was a pioneer in business and politics in Kentucky. They can look at what I've accomplished against big odds and say, "Well, if Mae Street Kidd can do it, so can I." I don't mean to brag, but in many

ways I've been a trailblazer, and young people tell me I've inspired them to work hard and accomplish something with their
lives. If I have helped only one young person become a success by my example, I'm proud of what I've done.

My most significant contribution as a role model, I think,
has been my dedication to hard work. When I was in the legislature, I'd get up early on Mondays and be on my way to
Frankfort by 7:30 in the morning. One day before I left I called
a politician friend and woke him up. He said, "Mae, what do
you mean calling me so early? I'm still in bed. It's too early to
get up." I said, "It's almost 7:30. The earlier you get up the
more work you can do. You can't work if you're in bed." Indeed, my work has been the most important single part of my
life. Every job I ever held I tried to do well. I never sat around
and waited for someone to tell me what to do. I was creative
and busy all the time. I not only met the requirements of my
job, but I tried to exceed them.

I've always called myself a salesman because, regardless of
the company or business or work I've done, I've tried to sell
something—a product, a service, a concept. People ask me now
for my secrets as a successful salesman. Let me count some of
my rules for success. First, I work hard and never give up. I
also do a lot of thinking and planning. I love people and enjoy
working with them. I want to prove myself. I'm fair to people
and I expect them to be fair to me. I'm not jealous of other
people and don't run them down. I'm friendly to people but
not mushy and sentimental. I am strictly business. I don't say
things I don't mean. People always know where I stand and
where we stand with each other. I'm very positive. I'm loyal to
the people and the companies I work for. While I'm working
for a company, I don't talk about it and try to tear it down. I'm
trustworthy. I've been lucky to have products and services and
causes to sell that were worthwhile. Whatever I've sold, I've
made sure it was exactly as I represented. What I'm selling
speaks for itself and it's also speaking for Mae Street Kidd. It's

representing me too. I never handled anything that could destroy my reputation.

I'm sorry now that I didn't have children, but I have been well recognized and honored for the service I've done for others. Of course, that hasn't been easy. I worked hard to get a good job or to get elected to public office. Then I might sit down and say, "Well, I'm somebody important now." But chances are that nobody thinks you're important but yourself. Many times you have to be dead before anyone recognizes you and honors you. I've been lucky to have received the honors and awards that I have. There are many people who are jealous of me and don't like to see me honored in any way. When names were being considered for the housing development in the Russell neighborhood, some people proposed my name, and it would have been Mae Street Kidd Place. But some people came and spoke against it! It was nothing but jealousy! No, it didn't bother me when they named it after someone who didn't deserve it, a Mr. Hampton that nobody knows anything about except he was a postman.

So right now there's nothing named for me in Louisville, but I'm pretty well known throughout the state. My picture is in the board room of the headquarters of the Urban League. Before they closed the Lincoln Institute, they named a girl's dormitory after me, and my name is also on the wall at the Kentucky Housing Corporation in Frankfort. Who knows? Maybe some day there will be a street or building or something named after me in Louisville, where I've lived most of my life. But you know what the Bible says about a prophet not having any honor in his own country.

A lot of streets in Louisville are named for whites and blacks who haven't done much, if anything, for this community. Muhammad Ali is an example. The so-called Louisville Lip has done very little to benefit his hometown. He doesn't even live in Louisville but somewhere up in Michigan. Cassius Clay, which was the name he was born with, grew up close to

Georgia Davis Powers, and she knows him a lot better than I do. I did know his parents quite well, especially his father. He was an artist who painted commercial signs, but he's dead now. Muhammad is a very successful man—and in many ways a very pitiful man because of his bad health condition. I just wish that he had done more for those people he left behind in Louisville. He has had the influence and the money to leave a wonderful legacy for his hometown, but about all he's done is say, "I'm from Louisville, Kentucky." Saying and doing are not the same.

Even Roy Wilkins, the national director of the Urban League, got his name on a street, and he didn't deserve that at all. I don't mean to say that only local people should have things named for them. Martin Luther King should be honored with a street. There was a movement started a few years ago to rename Chestnut Street for Dr. King, but most people living on my street objected, and it was dropped. So they named a little short downtown street for him. I did not want Chestnut renamed for him, but I think he deserves to be remembered with something more important than a street nobody knows.

I don't mean to sound dissatisfied and bitter with my own honors. I have received a lot of recognition. Sweetheart, this house wouldn't hold all the articles and mementos and honors I have. It's always nice to have somebody else say something good about you. Then you don't have to say it yourself! I have over a hundred awards now, and they're over in my collection at Kentucky State University in Frankfort. I've given a few items to the Western Branch of the Louisville Free Public Library, which has a large black history collection, but my main collection is at Kentucky State. They sent a van here twice and took most of my memorabilia, except for two albums I have here that are filled with clippings and photographs about my life and careers. I still have a few plaques on the wall in my living room from such organizations as the NAACP, the Kentucky Commission on Women, the National Conference of Christians and Jews, and the *Louisville Defender*. I can't even remember all the plaques I have. The May 1984 issue of *Ebony* cited me as a distinguished state legislator. In 1968 I received the Kennedy-King Award for dedication, diplomacy, and legislative skill in getting the open-housing bill passed in the General Assembly. Why, I've even been a guest in the White House! On Friday afternoon, September 21, 1979, I was Mrs. Carter's guest at a reception recognizing black officeholders. So you see I have received a vanload of awards, and I have kept a lot of stories and articles about my career. Eventually, all of them will go to Kentucky State because I want them protected and made available for historical research.

I hope that my life and work are a legacy worthy of remembrance. But after I've left some bequests to several relatives, I plan to leave the bulk of my estate to the Mae Street Kidd Scholarship Fund, which is managed by the Lincoln Foundation. It will provide money for deserving black students to go to college and take advantage of opportunities I didn't have. I've been building it up over several years. About a dozen young black professional women organized the Mae Street Kidd Auxiliary a few years ago to raise money for my scholarship fund. Every year they have a major benefit like a dance or a style show and have already donated several thouand dollars to the fund. They say they are dedicated to preserving my legacy. That makes me feel so good. They must like me a lot to be doing projects like that. Such good deeds help to balance the ill will of people who don't like me. Of course, I know that nobody can be in professional and public life as long as I have without making some enemies. The world will always have its bad people, but thank the Lord, there are good people to balance them.

I've been trying to build the scholarship fund up to $50,000, which would be a large enough principal to provide income for several grants each year. I go after money wherever I can find it. The Black Women's Coalition gave me $1,500 for the fund, and I got a large contribution from a local white businessman. He called me one day and asked me to do him a favor. I said, "Why is it that you never call me unless you want something?" He said, "Well, what can I do? I'd like to do something in your name." I said, "I know just what you can do. You can make a contribution to my scholarship fund at the Lincoln Foundation." I met him at a local restaurant, and he pulled out an envelope from his pocket with a check in it. I thought, "Well, it might be for $1,000, and that will be all right. I certainly won't turn my back on $1,000." To my great surprise and delight, however, when I opened the envelope, the check was for $10,000! Now, you know I cried a few happy tears over that. Every week I'm getting closer and closer to my goal.

Now I want to tell you about some of the people I have known and admired through my life. Some of them are famous and some are not. No one lives her life alone. Although I've made my own way through life most of the time, I have had good samaritans who have aided and inspired me when I needed them—sometimes from a distance. First, I'll name some well-known people who have crossed my path in a positive way. I've met and known many of the outstanding black leaders of our time, from Maynard Jackson, the mayor of Atlanta, to Arthur Ashe, the tennis player. I have a picture of me dancing with Mr. Jackson at the Galt House during an annual meeting of the Urban League. Twice I introduced Julian Bond when he came to Louisville to make speeches.

Two of my close friends were the two Whitney Youngs, Sr. and Jr. The father became the first African American to head Lincoln Institute in 1935, and he made it into a model school for blacks. Later, I was privileged to serve on the board of trustees under him. His son became national executive director of the Urban League and did a beautiful job as its leader. On a trip to Nigeria in 1971, he drowned while swimming in some shallow water. I have always been suspicious about his death, and so was his father. He was an excellent swimmer and in good health, and it doesn't make sense that he would have drowned. Until his own death, Whitney Sr. grieved over

Dancing with Maynard Jackson

his son's suspicious and untimely death. This father and son made a huge contribution to furthering race relations in this state and this country, and they were my friends.

Of course, I knew Martin Luther King Jr., but perhaps not as well as some people in Louisville. I think he was a great leader because he preached peaceful, nonviolent opposition to racial discrimination. A lot of people want to fight and burn and kill. That was not Martin's way. I was with him just about every time he came to Louisville, but he was always in a rush. He'd be in a parade or demonstration, make a speech, preach a sermon in his brother's church at Zion Baptist, and then run out to catch the plane to go to his next appearance.

I know about the rumors that he and Georgia Davis Pow-

ers had a close relationship. That is none of my business. When
the news broke that a black Kentucky legislator was with him
in Memphis when he was killed, a reporter called me and said,
"There were only two black women in the legislature at that
time—you and Georgia Davis Powers. Was it you?" I said, "I
am not the woman. I have been to Memphis, but I was not in
Memphis when Dr. King was killed." And I hung up.

I was not surprised that Dr. King was killed. I knew that
someday somebody would do it. That's what happens here in
America. When a black leader gets too popular and too influ-
ential, certain people will not let him live. He becomes an
automatic target. Sometimes I fear for Jesse Jackson, but I'm
sure of the risks he's taking. I like Jesse very much and have
supported his work financially. He's a good representative for
the black race. I've known him personally since he came to
speak to the Kentucky General Assembly, and I saw him several times when he came to speak in Louisville. I got to know
him fairly well. He called me Sister Kidd. I think he'd like to
be a congressman from the District of Columbia, but something must have happened between him and President
Clinton. The President hasn't pushed for DC statehood, and
I know that's a great disappointment to Jesse. The District has
a lot of problems and needs to become a state in order to solve
them. Jesse could be an eloquent and powerful spokesman for
the new state of Columbia or whatever they decide to call it.

You know, there are some people who have their own
unique language—people like Whitney Young Jr. and John
Kennedy. So does Jesse. It's good English but it's different and
inviting and sincere and filled with beautiful phrases. When
he speaks, you say, "Only Jesse Jackson speaks like that. He's
the only one." He pushes himself into unpopular, controversial positions on a lot of issues, but if he didn't he wouldn't get
anywhere and we wouldn't make any progress. Like Dr. King,
he has a vision for himself and his country, and he doesn't
worry about the danger it puts him in. When you go into public life, you take on risks. Fortunately, I've never been threat-

ened or in any real danger, even though I was always outspoken. I've never even received any hate mail or anonymous, obscene phone calls. I've been lucky.

Needless to say, a lot of white people have been good friends to the cause of civil rights for blacks, beginning with Abraham Lincoln. I've known and worked with many whites when we had a common cause to promote. But I must add quickly that blacks have had to fight their own battles. If blacks hadn't fought for their rights themselves, we wouldn't be where we are today. Nevertheless, we have been greatly aided by our white friends. Here in Kentucky I've known and worked easily with many white politicians, from the five governors under whom I served to several mayors of Louisville. Take Harvey Sloane, for instance. He was a medical doctor and came to Louisville to head the Park-Duvalle Heath Center in the West End. Later, he became a good mayor of the city, and I supported him because he seemed to want to do right by everyone. Then when he ran for the Democratic nomination for governor, I became his statewide co-chairman. Of course, I didn't like everything about him, but I liked him enough to want him to be governor. I thought he was better than the other candidates. We all have our lapses and inconsistencies, and so did he. I will never forget an incident that occurred during the campaign. He asked me to accompany him to Lexington for a campaign rally, and we flew in his helicopter out of Louisville and landed on the top of the new downtown hotel. We went down to the street level together, and then he did something very strange. He put me in one car and he left for our meeting in another car without me. I took that as a slight. If he hadn't wanted to be seen with me arriving at the rally in the same car, he should have left me in Louisville.

A white politician who is as open and sincere and honest and well-intentioned as they come is Jimmy Carter. I met him when he was governor of Georgia, and I was attending a meeting in Atlanta. Also attending were the black mayor of Atlanta, Andrew Young; the black mayor of Tuskegee; and Governor

George Wallace of Alabama in his wheelchair. We were all sitting at the head table, and Mr. Carter was down the row on my left. When the meeting was over, I spoke to all of them. To Mr. Carter I said, "Governor, will you give me your place card as a souvenir?" He said, "Of course, I will, and I'd like to write something on it." So he wrote, "For Mae Street Kidd, from a friend of Mayor Young."

When he became president and I was in Washington for a meeting of women in politics, we all went to the White House for a reception. He and Rosalynn were in the receiving line. When I got up to him, I said, "Mr. President, I know you don't remember me, but I met you in Atlanta at a banquet when you were governor, and you gave me your place card." He said, "Of course, I remember you, Mrs. Kidd," and smiled that broad, toothy smile of his. That's what I liked about him. He was plain and had the common touch. He could identify with real people. I really liked it when he and Rosalynn walked down the street at his inauguration. I liked his dedication to his wife and his family. He even stood behind his brother Billy when Billy was causing him all kinds of embarrassments. On the other hand, President Bush didn't have the common touch. He came from a rich family, and we don't need too many rich people as president. They can't understand how most of us live.

I've never met President Clinton, but I like him. He tries to do the right thing, but I think he compromises too quickly and needs to stand on his own two feet. I think Hillary is brilliant and is very supportive of her husband. In fact, I think she might make a better president than he is! But the one recent president that I really admire for what he accomplished was President Lyndon Johnson. To my regret, I never met him or Lady Bird. He did many wonderful things for civil rights and for the poor of all races in this country. I think it's especially fitting that he was from the South.

Louisville has been blessed with many good black leaders, and I've known them all during the past seventy years that

I have lived here. Some have been political leaders and others have made their reputations in sports, business, education, the arts, and other professions. I've known the black artist Ed Hamilton since he was a boy riding his tricycle down the sidewalk outside this house. He is a nationally known artist and has made magnificent statues of such black heroes as Joe Louis and Isaac Murphy, the black jockey who won the Kentucky Derby so many times. Of course, I know and respect my friend Georgia Davis Powers, who was an important voice for equality as a senator in the Kentucky General Assembly when I was in the House. The educator and civil rights leader Lyman T. Johnson and I belong to the same church, Plymouth Congregational. We're both strong-willed and plain-spoken. He knows who he is, and I know who I am. He has been on the front line at the barricades in the civil rights struggles, but he's never been a rabble-rouser. His struggles and methods were different from mine, but we had a common objective to see that justice was done. I admire him for his role in opening up the University of Kentucky to blacks and for leading sit-ins at downtown lunch counters. He was doing his work his way, and I was doing mine my way.

Now finally, I want to single out a few more people who have been important influences for me and have lived lives that I much admire. You'll excuse me if I name my mother first of all. I've already paid tribute to her elsewhere, but I can never honor her name adequately. She was the guiding light of my life. Next there was Aunt Nellie Henderson, with whom I sat on the swing and talked on lazy Sunday afternoons in Millersburg. She looked a lot like my mother. She was not as light as I am, but she was fair and had beautiful black hair. I learned more from her on that front porch swing than I would have learned ripping and running around like the other kids.

Another woman from my Millersburg girlhood was Mrs. Elizabeth Bowen, the principal of the black elementary school and a wonderful teacher. I've also paid my tribute to her elsewhere, but I can never say how much inspiration I gained from her. More recently, I should name Dr. Samuel Robinson, the president of the Lincoln Foundation in Louisville. Sam is genuine and dedicated to his job. Like me, he came up the hard way and achieved his place in the sun by working for it. When I was chairman of the Lincoln Foundation board, I found him easy to work with. He never got angry or upset even when someone disagreed with him.

The last two people I want to single out are whites—a man and a woman. Lee Thomas Jr. is the president of Thomas Industries, which manufactures lighting fixtures. He's a big businessman but is never too busy to help with good causes. He served on the Lincoln Foundation board for almost thirty years, like his father before him. I don't believe there's an ounce of prejudice in his body. He represents a lot of good white people who have helped blacks do their own work. You know, you can't do other people's work for them, but you can bring them a dipper of water while they do it. That's the role white people have played for black people.

Then there is a good white person named Anne Braden, a brilliant and brave woman who has helped black people as much as anyone I know. She took a stand for civil rights back when it was unpopular, even dangerous, to do so. She got into a lot of trouble with her support of open housing and busing and other forms of integration. People labeled her and her late husband Carl communists in 1954 after they bought a house in a white Louisville neighborhood and sold it to a black electrician named Andrew Wade IV. The house was shot up and even bombed before the black family was forced to leave. I've seen the house and I never thought it was anything to get killed over. It wasn't even brick.

The Wades were a high class of people and well educated. They were certainly above the caliber of the white neighborhood they tried to move into. Of course, they went there mainly to show that they should have the right to live anywhere they could afford to. That's the kind of legislation I succeeded in getting through the Kentucky legislature a quarter of a century later. It took a brave man to do what he did, and it took brave white people to stand behind him. I don't think I could have done it. As I say, they had their way of pushing for equal rights, and I had mine. Mr. Wade's son, by the way, is my electrician and came by just yesterday to repair my outdoor floodlights.

As long as we continue to have such well-intentioned people—and thousands and thouands more like them in Louisville, in Kentucky, and throughout this country—we can be assured that people will continue to be treated fairly, regardless of their race, religion, or sex. All the battles have not been won yet, and even the victories can be undone if we rest our guard. As Thomas Jefferson once reminded us, "Eternal vigilance is the price of liberty."

To close out these remarks, I will try to sum up my service to civil rights and show how it differs from other approaches by recalling an incident that occurred during a train trip through Mississippi in the 1950s. I was with a group of delegates returning from a meeting of the National Negro Insurance Association in California. We were in our special car and had stopped at a small Mississippi town when suddenly I heard a shot fired from outside the train toward us. It barely missed the president of one of our largest black insurance companies. When we saw that no one had been injured, someone said jokingly to me, "Come on, Mae. Let's go inside the train station and get us a soft drink and a sandwich. Don't you want to put your feet on Mississippi ground?" I said, "The hell I do." I had no intention of confronting a mad dog on his own ground. I had other ways to cage him.

Today's Problems,
Tomorrow's Solutions

Today everybody has problems—big problems. It's not just a black problem or a white problem. It's a universal problem. The general moral decay and lawlessness of our society have infected everyone, but none more deeply than the black community. Sometimes I almost despair when I count the troubles that afflict my people—joblessness, drugs, violence, promiscuity, the breakdown of the family, and disrespect for everything from language to authority. To some young people, a human life—their own or anybody else's—is worth no more than the insect you kill with the fly swatter.

I'll start with the family disarray because most of our problems can be traced back to the family, or I should say the lack of a family unit. I come from a nontraditional family. My white father never recognized his mixed-color children and, so far as I know, did very little to support us. Nevertheless, my mother and stepfather stepped in to fill that gap and did a superb job of raising us to work hard, respect authority, and to expect to reap what we sow. They instilled in us a sense of responsibility. Nowadays, in many black communities, families hardly exist. The single mother has children by several different boyfriends. She lives in government housing and is fed by food stamps and is clothed by welfare. What kind of self-respect can you have in a situation like that? What kind of environment is that for children to grow up in? What do they have to look forward to but another round of government handouts that barely keep body and soul together? To solve today's problems,

148

we have to do something quickly to strengthen the family. It may take some form of tough love, but it has to be radical. We've tried piecemeal reforms for a long time, and they don't work.

Look at the drug problem. Life is so bleak and dreary for people in the projects that they will turn to alcohol and crack and anything else that will lift their vision even temporarily. They don't value anybody's life—including their own. Human life has no more value than the rabbit or squirrel we run over in the car. The drug problem starts with little children getting on the school bus, and by the age of fourteen so many of them are addicted. Then addiction leads to burglaries and armed robberies because the drug habit is expensive to support. Because of the dope problem, living in a housing project is dangerous for everybody. Being a guard or a policeman in a project is risky work. Innocent people are often killed when they are in the line of fire between two drug dealers.

In many neighborhoods in Louisville, dope selling is out of control. It's a problem in white areas too. Our drug problems are not confined to one race or economic group. There is violence, drugs, illegitimacy among whites as well as blacks. The poor just start out with more problems. When you have money, you can hide some of your troubles. The poor white is in the same boat as the poor black. All poor people need help. They need help from society and they need to help themselves.

Almost all the bad things come out of the drug problem. A child thinks, "Why should I go to school when I can make a lot of money fast dealing drugs on the street?" That leads to violence. In many homes there are guns owned by the adults for legitimate purposes, but what on earth can a thirteen-year-old need with a gun? Or to phrase it a different way, what can he be doing that would make a gun necessary? If you live by the sword, you die by the sword. If you play with fire, you get burned. If you hang out with bad company, you will be bad. These warnings that we heard from our parents and teachers and preachers fall on deaf young ears today. To young people in the drug culture, they don't mean a thing. Some years ago I was visiting a friend in Chicago and we went to a party. As soon as we got inside the house and I saw people drinking and taking dope and becoming rowdy, I felt very uncomfortable. I said to my friend, "Come on. Let's get the hell out of here. I don't know these people, and I don't want to know them. They're not my people." I learned early in life that you will become like the people you associate with. There are some people you'd best keep your distance from.

The welfare system has also helped weaken the black family and black society. It has made too many people dependent—intelligent, able-bodied people who should be working at something. To begin with, young people should be required to stay in some kind of school until they learn enough to support themselves. Unfortunately, welfare has become a way of life for too many people. I know young children who stay at home from school on "check day" so they can get what they consider their "share" of their mothers' checks as soon as it arrives in the mail. I don't think young mothers should be rewarded for having more and more children. They should be rewarded if they get training for jobs so they can support themselves.

Sometimes I agree with the critics who say that the welfare system has become an incubator because it encourages and rewards single mothers—usually no more than children themselves—to have children, one child every nine months. Not all the money goes to the mothers and their children either. Their boyfriends often take their checks and foodstamps and buy cars and gas and clothes for themselves. I would say to the single mother after her first child: "We will help you with this child and maybe one more. But that's it. You must learn to protect yourself and to support yourself, or you will suffer the consequences." I'll bet the illegitimate baby population would decrease immediately.

We have to control the population some way, and I'm not

in favor of abortion on demand. Abstinence doesn't work. Young people are going to be sexually active. That leaves birth control as the only answer. God meant for us to procreate. That's one reason we're here on earth. But I think we're being over fruitful and multiplying too much. We shouldn't bring children into the world that we can't support.

Yes, I believe in some form of sex education, and it should ideally take place in the home. Unfortunately, most parents even today don't assume that responsibility, either because of ignorance or irresponsibility. In my generation parents didn't usually tell us about the birds and the bees. But when I was raising my half-sister, I resolved to be different. When she got to be about ten or twelve, I bought her books to read about birth. When she finished reading them, we talked about sex and childbirth. It was as natural as talking about the weather or the flowers and shrubs that grow in my yard. My sister Mary Evelyn said, "Mae, I know now why children ought to love their mothers. It's because the mother carries the baby around in her stomach for nine months and feeds it and protects it." When she got a little older, I talked to her about the boys in her school. I said, "Honey, you are a pretty girl, and the boys will want to talk to you and carry your books and try to kiss you. You should be friendly with them, but stay an arm's length away from them. Don't let them embrace you. Nature is funny. One thing leads to another. If you let a boy kiss you, it could wind up with sex. And sex can lead to a baby. And you're not ready to have babies. So keep your clothes on until you are married, and behave like a lady." I was always open and honest with her, and we never had any problems. She knew she could come to me if she had a question or got into trouble.

Most people laugh at me when I talk about the seriousness of another problem, and that is the inability of many blacks to use good English. Many, many blacks speak very bad English and even take pride in it. Some of them boast and call it Black English. I just call it Bad English. I don't think there's any justification for it. It is completely detestable. We are judged by what we wear—our clothes and our language. Yes, I think we wear our language just like a shirt or a dress. It communicates not only factual information but also attitudes, images, impressions. Bad grammar may communicate facts, but it also sends a negative message about the speaker. It says that a person who is sloppy in grammar and pronunciation will probably be sloppy in his work habits. Dirty clothes and unpolished shoes convey a negative image just like double negatives and mispronunciations. "I ain't got no pencil" states a fact very clearly, but it also says you may not be a good employee.

I know an intelligent young man in politics who talks in terrible English. I have tried to help him. Even his girlfriend has tried. But it's no use. He doesn't see the need for learning correct English. He says, "I'm doing all right just as I am. I don't need to speak any better." I said, "Yes, you've done very well, but it's in spite of your bad English. Think of how much better you could be doing if you improved your English. There will come a time when you will realize that your language is a serious handicap, and then it may be too late to do anything about it." He still didn't believe me, and I finally gave up trying to help him. He has some good ideas. He's nice looking and bright, but he will not be able to influence a lot of people with his bad English. He can go only so far, and he will be stopped. It's a shame.

I've heard blacks say, "Well, I talk like everybody I know. We all understand each other." That's my point. You will never be able to break outside that small group if you don't use good English. People say, "I can't help it if I speak bad English because that's the way people I know speak." That's a pitiful excuse. You can rise above that level. One of the women who works for me speaks atrocious English, and her grandchildren repeat exactly what she says. She is such a poor reader she makes me nervous. Because I can't see to read now, I ask her to read something for me, and she stumbles over so many words she can't pronounce, I lose track of what she's saying. It's so very sad. She has no excuse for not learning to speak and read and write better. She's had plenty of opportunities. It irritates the stew out of me to hear her mutilate the English language. It's so very sad. I feel sorry for her, but I feel worse for her grandchildren when they pick up her bad habits. She is condemning her own flesh and blood into a menial position all their lives. Their hope is to ignore what she teaches by example and rise above her. I say, "Even if your relatives and friends speak substandard English, you can do better. You can imitate the educated people you hear in school and church. It is easy to speak better English than your parents."

Black ministers are important role models for young black people, and many of them speak horrible English. They crack verbs and misuse pronouns and generally murder the language that blacks have been speaking for hundreds of years—in fact, a lot longer than a lot of white people in this country! The pastor we used to have at my church, Plymouth Congregational, is an exception. Dr. E. Alexander Campbell had a Ph.D. in theology and was an excellent speaker. Some of our members didn't care for his British accent, which was natural for him because he was from Jamaica. They said he was haughty and looked down on the congregation. I don't think that was true at all. His accent did set him apart from the rest of us, but I thought he was a wonderful pastor and set a good example for our youth.

Most of the black people I knew when I was growing up in Millersburg spoke good English, in fact, a lot better than most of the poor whites. The reason was that they often worked at the military institute and the girls' junior college, where they heard good language used. They never went around using bad grammar and saying "dis" and "dat" and using the wrong word forms. My mother always spoke good English. She was around a lot of well educated whites and picked up their language. Some poor whites worked at the military academy and the junior college and were around other educated whites, but I don't believe it rubbed off on them as much as it did on blacks. The blacks were always listening and then imitating. My full brother

George, who was as white as any white man in Bourbon County, couldn't stand poor whites. He had contempt for their lack of education, their lack of culture, their laziness.

There has always been a certain friction between blacks and poor whites. I think some of that friction comes from the fact that educated blacks in the professions felt superior to the uneducated whites, and the whites knew how they felt. Poor whites, however, were allowed to go to theaters and restaurants and schools that not even a black Ph.D. or M.D. could go to. On the one hand, poor whites were told by society and the laws that they were superior to all blacks, but on the other hand, they could look around them and see that they were inferior to many blacks by ability, by education, and by profession. It was so obvious that many blacks in Millersburg were better educated, spoke better English, had better manners, and more culture than many of the poor whites. Sometimes I felt really sorry for them. It was a shame to see how they had to live and raise their children. Sometimes I even think they are discriminated against. They need as much help as poor blacks, but they don't always get it. Poor blacks usually get more attention than poor whites—from the government, from social agencies, and from everybody else. So many poor whites are left to sink further into poverty.

The bottom line is that I don't see any defense of substandard English at all, whether it's used by blacks or whites. In particular, blacks should avoid so-called Black English like the plague. I don't care what its origins are. In fact, if its roots are in slavery and segregation, then that's all the more reason to do away with it. We have taken off those chains of oppression. It's high time we took off the language chains too. If we expect to compete successfully in a highly competitive society, we blacks must play by the rules that everyone else plays by. There can be no special rules just for us. Black leaders who say that black students should be judged on their ability to use Black English are dead wrong. You don't have to prove that you're black by speaking bad English. You are playing in the wrong ballpark, and you're playing in the minor leagues all alone. The lights are about to go out. Then you'll be in the ballpark in the dark.

Good English doesn't necessarily mean big words. It means standard grammar—the kind you should have learned in the seventh grade. It means a basic vocabulary of understandable English words. It means the pronunciation you can find in any dictionary. If I were interviewing a person for a job, and he spoke any kind of off-brand English, I'd classify him unsuited for the job. He could be white or black or yellow or brown or green. His color would have nothing to do with my decision. I would make my decision based on what was good for my business.

I have always tried to use good English, whether I'm speaking or writing. I have read writers who practice good English, and I have imitated speakers who know how to use the language. When I write poetry, I don't use so-called Negro dialect. I write in the language of the American poets I admire, like Longfellow, Whittier, Emerson, and Lowell. You may call my poetry a bit old-fashioned, but I don't mind. I can say by heart a poem I wrote a long time ago called "Thanksgiving":

> Oh God, Who rules the universe,
> Give us strength to carry on
> In Thy Name in a Thanksgiving way.
> Grant that we may ever hold fast
> To the teachings of Thy Will,
> That peace, love, and harmony
> In our hearts will instill.
> Keep us from want and care,
> And guide us in Thy Light
> That we may have favor in Thy sight.
> Oh God, today we do give thanks for these and more,
> For in tomorrow's dawn, the whole world must Thee adore.

I recited this poem at a meeting last summer of the Kentucky Housing Corporation in Frankfort, where I was guest of honor.

I was telling the audience how thankful I was for what God had allowed me to do with my life, and I said, "I wrote a poem that expresses what I feel. I'll try to repeat it." Well, I said it without missing a word. When I finished, all six hundred people in the audience stood and applauded. I certainly don't mean to hold my poem up as a model of great poetry, but it is at least written in clean, clear, understandable English.

There are many good models among contemporary black writers that should inspire young blacks. What about Maya Angelou, who read a beautiful poem at President Clinton's inauguration? What about Alice Walker, whose *Color Purple* was not only a successful novel but was made into a wonderful movie? What about Ernest J. Gaines, whose stories about his people in Louisiana show how the poor and oppressed can rise to victory? And what about Toni Morrison, who won the Nobel Prize for literature several years ago? Indeed, there are many, many good role models for blacks who want to use good English.

Role models are people we look up to and pattern ourselves by. They can be our parents, our friends, or they can be people from the front pages of the newspaper or from history books. From slavery times we look up to Sojourner Truth and Phillis Wheatley. Sojourner stole slaves and ran them through the Underground Railroad to freedom in the North and Canada. Phillis was a fine poet who had been brought to America from Africa. A remarkable woman from our own time is Rosa Parks, who refused to give up her seat on a Montgomery bus. Her story reminds me of a lady I know who used to work as an insurance agent for Mammoth Life and Accident Insurance Company. The woman was very overweight and wore very large, full dresses. She carried her policies in a basket, which she held in her lap when she sat down. One day she got on a Louisville street car and sat down in the first vacant seat, which happened to be next to a young white woman. The white girl immediately got up in a huff and moved to another seat. My friend looked over to her and said, "Oh, thank you so much, honey. I'm fat and tired. You're so sweet to give me more room." And she proceeded to spread her dress out over the entire seat and occupy all of it. I love to tell that story because she humiliated the bigoted white girl by pretending to thank her for a good deed.

We're never going to solve all our problems. We're never going to eliminate all prejudice and hatred based on race or religion or anything else. But we must try. As long as we live we must try to leave the world a better place than we found it—even if it's only in the small corner that we occupy. As I look into the future, I don't see any grand plans that will bring paradise down to earth. I can only throw out a few observations, beginning with solving economic inequalities. We must let people work on an even field. We must return to a respect for self-discipline and community discipline. We need to restore the church and the school to their rightful places in our society. Both institutions must take on greater responsibilities for helping young people develop into responsible adults with better facilities and expanded programs. The schools are being called on to do the work parents used to do, and that's a shame. But I don't see another institution that we can turn to for help. In the schools children can learn how to deal with anger and settle disputes without violence. Through the schools we can reach inner-city children and provide them with cultural and recreational opportunities. Of course, the churches can do similar work, but the schools can reach everyone, and they have more resources to work with.

We all need a better self-image, blacks in particular. We blacks must leave our slave mentality on the wasteheaps of history. We need pride in ourselves, but a healthy pride based on true self-worth. Children must be taught that education and hard work will pay off. A woman I know told me recently that her son used to drive a sanitation truck, and he made pretty good money. But he wanted a better job, so he started to night school and studied computer management. Now he has a good job with a big corporation, and he's making twice what he made on the garbage truck. More important than his enlarged salary is the fact that he has more pride in himself and what he's doing with his life. He may be the best role model I could hold up for young blacks today.

The keys, therefore, to a bright future for blacks are education, discipline, and hard work. We have to produce. We have to support each other. Parents have to take responsibility for their children and make them stay in school and study. The daughter of a friend of mine was arguing with her mother the other day about not being allowed to watch TV or to go to a party because she had school work to do. The girl said, "Well, I'll do like a boy in my class. He stayed at home." The mother said, "Why didn't he go to school?" She said, "Because he stayed up late watching TV and overslept." The mother said, "That's the lesson you will learn. You will stay home and not go to the party and not watch TV until your lessons are all done. Then you will go to bed and get up tomorrow morning and go to school." The daughter knew her mother meant business. We need more parents like that mother. Black parents need to discipline their children more. The problems start at home, and they can be solved at home. Black parents could learn a thing or two from my mother. She was a strict disciplinarian who told you to do something one time. The second time she told you with my stepfather's razor strap. After a couple of whippings, we obeyed her the first time.

Sometimes even good ideas can have negative consequences. This may sound odd, but I think there has been some negative fallout from desegregation. For one thing, our traditionally black colleges and universities are under attack and some are being closed in the name of efficiency. Several years ago there was a movement to close Kentucky State University in Frankfort. That would have been a terrible mistake. Blacks need to hold on to those parts of their past. The schools should be open, of course, to everyone, but they should retain their historic black identity in some way—perhaps with a good black studies curriculum or a black history collection in the library or a strong black component on the faculty.

In some ways integration has hurt professionals in the black community. In the old days, black lawyers, doctors, dentists, and other professionals had ready-made practices because blacks were frequently not welcomed in white offices. With desegregation many blacks lost their clients and patients. Blacks deserted their own people in droves. They seemed to think that whites were better prepared than blacks. I have white and black doctors and lawyers. I've tried to patronize black professionals when I could. I don't go to a white man because he's white. I don't go to a black man because he's black. I try to choose the person who's best for me. In earlier times we patronized other blacks because we had to. Now we should patronize them because they are good at their professions.

I have serious reservations about affirmative action because it implies that the group being helped is inferior. I think everybody ought to be treated equally. I doubt if, in the long run, affirmative action really helps women or minorities. If I were a white male, I wouldn't like for someone to get a job or be promoted over me solely because he or she was a woman or a black. People should get jobs and be rewarded according to their abilities. With the laws now on the side of equal opportunity, I don't think we need race- or gender-based jobs and promotions.

Blacks also need to work together more closely. We need to learn how to pool our money and our economic clout and use it like the Cubans in Miami or the Jews everywhere in the country. These people know how to stick together. We don't. We're too jealous of one another. We people of color must stop looking down on someone because his skin is lighter or darker than someone else's. Like Jesse Jackson's Rainbow Coalition, we have to love and honor everyone, regardless of his skin color or shade of color. Look at how the Jews have thrived in this country. Look at what they have done with Jewish

Hospital here in Louisville. They have built it into one of the biggest and best hospitals in this part of the country. They have done it because they know how to work together. We could learn a lot from the Jews. They know how to make a dollar out of a dime.

Of course, the Jews don't have the burden of slavery that we have—at least not in modern times. They have more self-confidence. We blacks don't have a good self-image. We don't believe we can do anything. I think the black pride movement is going in the right direction. The other day I was talking with a lady friend and her son, and he said, "Miz Kidd, I want to tell you what I learned at school today." I said, "Good. Tell me." He said, "I am somebody. If I think I can, I can. I am somebody." This little black boy was learning something very important. It was something that blacks of all ages need to know: If you think you can do something, you can do it because you are somebody important. I believe that's why I have been successful. I have always believed that I could do anything I wanted to do if I tried hard enough.

I am encouraged, however, by the opportunities that blacks have today. I took my car to Perkins Motors yesterday to leave it overnight for servicing. The young man who drove the shuttle to bring me home was black. It was the first time I'd ever seen a black person working there doing anything—not even cleaning up. He was a beautiful young man. He goes to church, and he has a group of young children that he teaches. He's a Big Brother and helps care for a young boy who doesn't have a father. That young man impressed me so much. He's showing us all what a person can do to improve himself and his community at the same time. This morning when he came and took me back to Perkins to pick up my car, I paid my bill to a very attractive young black woman. She was very efficient and looked happy. While I was talking to her, a young black man dressed in a neat suit walked over and said, "Mrs. Kidd, I'm Roosevelt, who used to go to school to Mr. Kidd. I work here now selling cars." I said, "Oh, Roosevelt, I'm so happy to see you working here." I congratulated him, then said to the woman with me, "This is all a revelation to me. For the first time, I've seen three young black people working here at responsible jobs. They're becoming successful." I almost felt like calling Mr. Perkins and thanking him for giving these young people a chance. But I realized of course that he was a smart businessman who had hired good workers who just happened to be black.

That kind of experience encourages me about the future for black people. On one side, I see the housing projects crammed full of unemployed people and children running wild without supervision. On the other side—even in the projects—are the parents who are strict and raise up smart, hardworking kids. Every year I go to the Black Achievers Banquet, where we recognize the achievements of black students. It makes me proud to see these young people getting grants and scholarships for college. It shows that black children, when given a chance, can compete with white children. Color has nothing to do with ability. The key to success is attitude. The parents make the difference, whether they are black or white. Success begins at home in the family.

All my life I have been called by various names—a Negro, a black person, an African American, a woman of color—all terms to set me off from other Americans. Call me what you like, but I like to call myself simply an American. I do not feel any particular kinship with Africa or Africans. The slave trade is a dark page of American history, but I wasn't around when it was going on, so I have no firsthand knowledge of it. I am simply an American with about 20 percent African blood, but I know little about Africa. I was not born in Africa, and neither were my parents or grandparents or ancestors going back for many, many generations. I have never been to Africa and have no more desire to go there than a white American whose ancestors came from France or Germany or Wales two hundred or more years ago.

Most of us, whether white or black, are mixtures of many

races and nationalities. We all have tangled roots. In fact, if I were to want to trace my roots, I don't know which parts of Europe and Africa I would go to. How can I, then, go back to my roots? I've got a little Indian in me, some Dutch, some Irish, some Welsh, maybe even some Jewish. I'm a melting pot all by myself. My ancestors, black and white, have been in this country a long, long time—much longer than most whites can claim. So I claim to be an American—period! I am not an African American or an Irish American or a Welsh American or a Native American. Since I was a girl, I have exercised my freedom to choose the course of my life because I am an American citizen. I still claim that right. I don't want anyone to make decisions for me until I am incompetent to make them myself. I don't want a doctor to try to send me to a nursing home without my permission. I will make all my own decisions as long as I can. After all, this is America.

Even with all its past and present faults, America is still the hope of the world. We have everything in this country that we need to make it work. We're ahead of every other country in every way I can think of. We've got brains. We've got material wealth. We've got experts who know how to do things. A nation that can put a man on the moon and bring him back can do anything on earth. We've got a president who is trying to get us to work together. We have millions of people of good will who want to make this nation work. Indeed, we have a bright and glorious future. America is still the best country in the world. Moreover, I think Kentucky is just about the best state to live in. We have good people and good laws, a beautiful country, abundant resources. The races get along very well. I don't know of any other place where life is better.

Living in the Nineties

When you get my age, you think a lot about where you've been, and you begin to think about what you have left. By any measure of longevity, I've been very lucky. Until my stroke and heart attack and eye problems, I've had no serious illnesses. When I was in my twenties, my heart doctor discovered that I had a heart murmur, but he was able to control it with medicine and rest. Nowadays, doctors want you to keep active even with a weak heart, but back then I was put to bed periodically for three or four weeks at the time to rest. It was never a big problem, but my heart condition was always lurking in the background, and I checked in with my doctor every month. Just recently I've had a pacemaker implanted, but everything seems to be going smoothly. My heart condition has been a disturbing background presence in my life, and I think it gave me an urgency and a zest for life—a feeling that I should not waste my time. Living in the shadow of death has caused me to live an active, productive life. I've taken care of myself, exercising and eating the right kinds of food. I've never smoked or used tobacco in any form. I'm not a drinker, though I do like an occasional glass of champagne. My doctor has told me to drink a little wine to whet my appetite. Right now I don't think I have any wine or champagne in the house. I couldn't afford to buy many luxuries any more because I have four people on my payroll and I have to keep this house up. Even if I wanted to, I can't afford to be drinking and smoking my money up.

My health problems really started with my eyes. I had a

cataract taken off, and that caused a bad hemorrhage. Soon my vision got bad in both eyes. I wanted so much to have my normal vision back, and my doctor referred me to a specialist in Louisville who did another operation on the retina with the help of two interns. Actually, the interns did the operation, and they didn't know what they were doing. They really botched the operation and left me legally blind. When they finished with me, my eyes were like scrambled eggs. I realize now too late that I should have left well enough alone, but I wanted the best. The result was that I have almost no sight at all. Before the operation I could read the name and addresses and phone numbers in a directory that the Center for the Blind gave me. Since the operation, I can't see anything in it. I know that a lot of the blame is mine, but doctors are supposed to know more about the eyes than I do. One of them should have said, "Mrs. Kidd, this is a risky operation. Any time you work on the retina, you're in danger because the retina is your eyesight. If it is injured, you don't see. Be careful if you let anyone touch your eyes." I'm not bitter toward my doctor. In fact, I've had a letter written to him saying I didn't blame him for what happened to me. However, he should have warned me!

I have been almost hysterical at times about being trapped in darkness. I've tried everything to get some remedy. I've made the rounds of eye doctors, but they can do nothing. They say, "Well, your sight will never be any better or any worse." That's no comfort at all! I am blind! I can't read. I can't drive my car. I can't take care of my house and yard. How much worse can it get? I am trapped like an animal.

My heart problems started with my eyes. I was grieving about my eyes, and then my brother Webster died in May of 1991. He had come to see me from Dayton and was helping me move some furniture. He said he wasn't feeling well, and he cut short his visit and went home. Two days later I called him, and his wife said he was in the hospital with lung cancer. He had been a heavy smoker all his life. Five weeks later, surrounded by his loving family, he died. All my sorrows were piling up.

About three months after my brother died, I was coming down my stairs when something told me to call my neighbors, the Joseph Carrolls, down the street. It was on a Sunday morning. The night before I had felt well enough to write a short piece for the *Louisville Defender*. But now I was feeling very strange. I stood at the bottom of the steps with my hand on the railing, and I picked up the phone from my desk. I don't know who answered the phone, but I said, "Hello, this is Mae. Please come to my house. I think I'm having a stroke." How in the world I knew I was having a stroke I'll never know. Then suddenly my knees gave way, and I was sitting on the floor right by the desk.

Mr. Carroll told me later he called an ambulance immediately, and he and his wife rushed to my house. The house was locked up tight, and nobody could get in because I couldn't move to open a door. Soon I heard the ambulance arrive and people began gathering outside. I could hear them calling, "Mrs. Kidd. Mrs. Kidd. Are you all right?" I could talk but I couldn't move. Mr. Carroll knew how careful I am about my house, but he came up to the door on my side porch and said, "Mae, I'm going to have to break a window pane in your big French door so we can get in." I said, "Hurry up and break it!"

There I am, sitting inside on the floor unable to move. I can't even crawl. I make an effort to move and I can't. But I can hear the people talking outside and understand what they're saying. I said, "Now when you break the glass, put your hand through and reach around and you'll find the key in the lock. Turn the key and push the latch back, and the door will open." In less than a minute he was in the house and opening the doors so the ambulance people could bring in their stretcher. I said, "Now, please go upstairs to the first door on the right. That's my bedroom. Look in the chair and bring my pocketbook down here to me." He brought it to me and I said,

"Look in the corner of the pocketbook and you'll find the keys to my car and to my house. Give them to your wife to keep for me. Make sure my pocketbook gets to the hospital with me."

The medic who came with the ambulance said, "Please, Mrs. Kidd, I've got to get you to the ambulance so we can put you on oxygen." I said, "I've got to do what I've got to do. Then I'll be ready." Finally, after I had given a few more directions, I said, "All right, I'm ready now." They took me outside and rushed me to Jewish Hospital, and in no time somebody put a phone to my ear and a voice said, "Mae, this is Dr. Morris Weiss. Everything is all right. I'll take care of you." I said, "All right." He said, "Don't worry about a thing." I said, "I won't." Later, one of his patients told me that she was in his office when the call came that I was in the hospital with a stroke, and he said to her, "I'm sorry, but I have to leave you. Mae Street Kidd's in the hospital, and I have to go to her immediately." Of course, he's my family doctor and a heart specialist; so he had no choice but to come.

I never lost consciousness. I was awake and aware all the time I was being taken to the hospital. I heard somebody say, "Listen to Mrs. Kidd. That woman hasn't stopped talking since they put her in the ambulance. She's telling everybody what to do!" Sam Robinson, my friend who's president of the Lincoln Foundation, was standing nearby and said, "That's like her. She's just tending to business."

Soon I began to get confused. I remember arriving and being taken to a beautiful room, and then I lost track of time. A couple of days after the stroke, I had heart failure, and then I had a heart attack. I remember the doctors were pushing people out of the room, and somebody was trying to get me to respond. I could hardly breathe and became unconscious. One of the doctors told me later he thought I was gone. I don't remember any of that. I do remember that sometime during that period I had a nightmare.

I dreamed I was in the hospital in bed, and there were

some Oriental people working there who were trying to spy on the United States. Somehow I knew they were spies and were trying to steal information about the patients from the hospital files. They had boxes of information packed and were just about ready to escape with the secrets, when they realized that somebody knew about their plot. They had their bags packed and were ready to leave when they discovered that I was the one who knew what they were up to.

Suddenly, I became aware that my wrists and ankles were taped to the bed, and some women were taking the rings off my fingers. A little old dried-up Oriental man came into the room and I said, "Are you going to kill me?" He didn't say anything. Then I saw that they also had Mr. and Mrs. Carroll and were going to take them as hostages. There is a long time when a lot of people were coming and going, and I wasn't sure what was going to happen to me. I couldn't help myself because I was taped to the bed. Finally, the old man said he wouldn't kill me, and all the spies left the building, and I woke up surrounded by my friends and family and lovely flowers all over the room.

I know that my nightmare was tied in with my heart troubles. I was vaguely aware during this time that my hands had swollen, and a jeweler had to be called in to cut my rings off my fingers. Of course, I also knew I was unable to do anything for myself; and that was like being tied to the bed. For the first time in my life, I was totally helpless, and that was enough to make me have a terrible nightmare.

I had excellent and loving care while I was in the hospital, but it was a crushing ordeal. One morning I developed cramps in both my legs, and they were hurting so bad I thought I had to get up and leave. I called a nurse and said, "I can't stand this pain any longer. I've got to get out." The nurses held me down and tried to calm me, and the doctor walked in and gave me a shot to reduce the pain. I began losing weight and soon had lost twenty-nine pounds. I stayed in the hospital for about two weeks; then I was transferred next door to the Frazier

Rehab Center for physical therapy for six weeks. I couldn't walk and my left hand was paralyzed.

The first day in rehab the nurses got me up on my feet, but I was unable to put one foot in front of the other. I was like a baby learning to walk all over, but I was determined that I would not be an invalid the rest of my life. With a nurse on either side of me, I tried and tried; and they clapped every time I made progress. It's very, very hard to relearn to use your limbs; but I can get around pretty well now, even though I still don't have full use of my left hand. That's the only part of my body that seems permanently affected. I have to wear a glove on it, and when I take it off, my hand gets cold.

Finally, Dr. Weiss told me I had made sufficient progress to leave the hospital. He wanted me to go to a nursing home. I said, "I don't want to go to a nursing home." He said, "Mae, just try it for ten days and see how you like it. It's comfortable and convenient for you, but if you want to go home later, you can." I already knew that I couldn't stay at home by myself and without help, and I had arranged to have the services of a practical nurse. She had come to the hospital several times to visit and told me how much she wanted to take care of me. Reluctantly, however, I had agreed to give the nursing home a try. On the day I was to leave the hospital, my private nurse and Mr. Carroll came to take me to a nursing home on the outskirts of town.

When we arrived, the attendants put me in a wheelchair and pushed me inside a huge, rambling building with long halls and row after row of rooms. They pushed me first down this hall and then down that hall, and my head began to swim. As they were wheeling me up and down the corridors, I saw women wringing their hands and pulling their hair and hollering, screaming, and crying. Finally, we got to my room and I looked inside and saw a woman sitting up in her bed whimpering. I couldn't take any more, and I cried, "Stop it! Take me home. I will not stay in this place another minute. It is a madhouse, and it will drive me mad." Everybody looked at me in shock. They weren't used to having anyone react this way. The manager came up to see what all the commotion was about. I said, "Did you hear me? Take me home. And I mean take me home right now."

I think everyone was so stunned that no one questioned my orders. The attendants wheeled me around and we started back to the entrance the way we came, with everyone looking at us as we went up and down the halls. When we got to the front desk, the lady assistant manager came over. I took her hand and put my other hand behind her head, pulled her down to me, and kissed her on the cheek, and said, "Goodbye." I was ready to go home. I had made no preparations to go home at all, but I knew my beds were made and my house was clean because that's the way I kept it and left it. I knew where everything was. I could have found my way around my house blindfolded. When we got to the house, my nurse called her son to come get her so she could get some clothes and move in with me. She stayed with me for six months and did what she was supposed to do—which was to cook and set the table and help me bathe and dress. She didn't do any housekeeping because I already had a cleaning woman.

I never regretted leaving that nursing home and coming to my real home. If they hadn't taken me home when I demanded it, I would have left by myself—even if I'd had to crawl all the way. I couldn't take all that hollering and screaming and crying. I have not been back since I left, and I don't plan to if I can help it. I resumed my normal life, and the following Sunday I was at church and I haven't missed a service since. When I say my life returned to normal, I don't mean that I could do everything I used to do before I lost my eyesight and before I had my stroke and heart attack. The stroke affected even my voice. It did something to my throat and made my voice husky. It has weakened me and forced me to be very cautious when I move around. Even so, I've had a lot of falls. When I get up to anwer the doorbell, I sometimes trip over a rug or a piece of furniture. The stroke left permanent damage to my left hand, which is paralyzed, though with therapy I've learned to move my fingers a little. The stroke also weakened my left leg, which I tend to drag a bit, but I exercise by walking back and forth between the hall and kitchen, maybe 130 times a day. But I'm still not able to jump rope! I don't suppose I'll ever be able to do that again.

I've tried to follow my doctors' orders carefully. For example, I drink some quinine every day to help prevent another stroke. But I'm fed up with arrogant doctors! When I was a girl, I had the measles and chicken pox and was left with some hearing loss in my left ear. But lately, I've had some increased hearing problems, and I went to an ear doctor. He said I had nothing wrong except some wax in my ear. I may have had a little wax in my ear, but that was not the cause of my problem. I am tired of dealing with doctors who are arrogant, insensitive, and incompetent.

Here's another example. One night I fell and broke a little bone in my right hand. My regular doctor put a little piece of cardboard over the hand to hold it, but it wasn't fixed right. It wasn't a proper cast. When it got to bothering me later, I went to the emergency room and had a good cast put on it. But it was too late. The hand had already grown back crooked. The first doctor had made a terrible mistake at my expense. When I told him about it, he was rude and despicable. You see why I don't trust doctors any more. They will hurt you about as much as they help you. Sometimes they will hurt you even more! What's more, they charge for it!

I'm trying to make the best of my condition and the time I have left in this life. But I don't know when something new will strike. I don't know when something unexpected will happen to my body tomorrow or next week or next month. I have to live day by day and try to make the most of every day. I have to live out my days in this house. It's my home and home is where I want to be. I don't ever want to return to a hospital or have to go to a nursing home. I have a lot of friends who check on me. They call me and they come and take me for rides in

their cars. I'm on the go all the time, and that's what I like. If I
stay at home, I brood and worry about my condition. I'd go
crazy if I had to sit here and twiddle my thumbs.

I get up at six o'clock every morning. The girl who gets
my breakfast helps me dress if I need her. She comes three
days a week and another woman comes three days, and on
Sunday the woman across the street comes over to help me.
She makes sure I'm dressed right for church when the chairman of our board of deacons picks me up at 10:30. After church
I go out with friends to eat dinner, and we spend the afternoon driving around. I like to stay out of the house on Sunday as much as I can because I'm pretty much housebound
the rest of the week when other people are at work.

I have four people on my payroll—the two women who
help me on weekdays and one on Saturday, plus a yardman
who cuts the grass, pulls up weeds, and rakes. I don't expect
people to do work for me for nothing. My monthly expenses
come to $3,300, which is a large amount for me. Until I got
sick, if I wanted something, I bought it. I'd never been accus-
tomed to scrimping before, but now I have to be very careful.
I still pay for what I get, but I can't afford to overpay. But let
me tell you about an incident that happened just a week ago
after church. Two friends and I went over to Huber's Restaurant in Starlight, Indiana, and had a $12 dinner. When I put a
dollar down for a tip, one of my friends said, "Mae, that's not
enough. Put down another dollar." I said, "If each of us puts
down one dollar, that's three dollars. It seems to me that's
enough for what the waitress did for us. We didn't ask for extra
service. She just brought the food to the table. I know a white
man who is a millionaire, and I've seen him tip thirty-five
cents." She said, "Well, if you can't afford to tip, you shouldn't
come here." Imagine that! It really upset me. I've always been
very liberal with people who work for me. That's one reason I
don't have much now. I was shocked that a woman who's supposed to be a friend would talk to me like that.

I like to go to the Quality Restaurant over on Jefferson

Street because it's quiet, and they have good food and good service. The other day I took one of my lady employees with me for a sandwich, and I left a dollar and a quarter for a tip. That shows how generous I am! That's very generous for a blind woman in my condition with four people on her payroll. I think my friend who called me down at Huber's is a show-off. She likes to embarrass people in public.

My income is fixed, and I have to account for every dime. It comes from several sources, including a small pension. I also have a few investments and I get Social Security. Of course, I have a few assets that I can sell in case of an emergency. I could sell my antique furniture, but I hope I don't have to. The company I bought the piano from said they would buy it back for what I paid. Of course, that's not much money since I bought it a long time ago for my sister to use when she took lessons. I have a silver service for eight which I have tried to sell, but the market for silver isn't good right now. You see, I don't mean to be stingy. I try to pay my own way and be fair to everybody, but I have to count all my pennies. Don't misunderstand me. I don't want you to feel sorry for me. I'm not complaining about my finances. I'm lucky to be living at home and to be able to afford to have people look out after me.

When I go out or when I have company at home, I try to fix myself up. I don't want anybody seeing me looking like a bum. Even at my age and in my condition, I'm still concerned about my appearance. I don't see well, but I can still put on my make-up. A woman said to me the other day, "Mae, I can see how to use a mirror, and I can't put on my make-up like you. The way you put your lipstick on you'd think you had a mirror right in front of you. You have a perfect mouth." With my hand paralyzed like it is, the only thing I can't do is comb my hair by myself. What I'm saying is that I will not go out in public unless I look good. I will not have people looking at me and saying, "There's poor old Mae Street Kidd. She's just let herself go to ruin. She doesn't look good like she used to."

As much as I've tried to accept my condition and adjust to

it, I find it very hard to accept. People say, "Well, you've had a long and rich and meaningful life." I say, "I'm still upset. I'm still angry. I am forced to live in a different world and I don't like it." People say, "Well, you know there are people worse off than you are." I say, "So what! That news doesn't bring me back my eyes. It's hard to be worse off than not being able to see!" Right or wrong, that's the way I feel. It's so hard to change your way of life. I've been an independent woman all my life, and I don't like to be restricted in any way. I want to be in control of my destiny. I have been developing claustrophobia. I don't like a door closed on me. I don't want to be locked in a car. And being blind is like being locked in permanently, and it bothers and hurts me more than I can possibly say. I am outraged by my condition, even while I try to accept it.

I am outraged by having to live in a dark world by myself. Recently, I was out with a group of younger women in their forties. They were so good and helpful to me. They led me to my seat. They fixed my food. They were friendly and included me in their conversation. They did everything to make me feel like a member of the group. Yet I still felt like I was in a distant world, light-years away from them. There was nothing they could do about it, and nothing I could do about it.

Most of my pleasures in life have been taken from me. I can't enjoy my beautiful home as much as I did. I can't drive my wonderful car—my Chrysler Fifth Avenue with red leather upholstery. When it's driven I have to pay someone else to do it. It's an '86 with only 16,000 miles on it and is worth over $20,000. But it's worthless to me now. It's like my house and my body and my mind. They don't mean much when you can't use and enjoy them.

I had planned to do so much more with my life, and now I can hardly do anything. I know that God is not pleased with my attitude, and I've tried to talk to Him about it. He seems to say, "Didn't Job suffer with no explanation? Didn't he suffer worse than you have?" And I answer, "Yes, Lord, I know he did." Still, I find myself asking, "Why me? Why me, Lord?"

Passing for Black

Despite my dominant white features, I have been classified as a black person all my life. I have lived as a black and have had to accept second-class citizenship. I never made an issue of my color or race, and when I was off by myself and no one knew my racial identity, I lived like a first-class American citizen. I went where I wanted to go. I did what I wanted to do. Nobody asked any questions. I never wore a badge saying, "Look at me! I'm Black!" Some people might call that "passing," but I don't. I was simply living my life as myself. I never tried to "pass" for white or black. If people want to know what I am, I say, "I'm an American citizen." That should be enough identity. I hope that all this race superiority business is behind us. I don't want anybody to say that any color or race is superior to any other. We are all different, but that doesn't make one person or group superior to another.

Like all Americans who are classified as blacks, I have been discriminated against—not just by whites but by other blacks. Those of us who are light-skinned African Americans have had to carry a special burden through life. Blacks can be resentful of each other. Darker ones often feel that there is a caste system and we lighter ones have advantages. Indeed, blacks with white fathers—or mothers—were sometimes given support by their white parents. That meant that they were sent to good schools and were more likely to get into one of the educated professions—the law, medicine, dentistry, education, the ministry. If you look through the pages of yearbooks of predominantly black colleges in the South from about 1880 on down to the end of segregation in the 1950s, you will see that a large percentage of the students are light-skinned. That means, of course, that one of their parents—usually the father—was white. White fathers sometimes sent their illegitimate children on to college. That was an advantage that darker blacks did not have and led to some resentment.

I never had that advantage. My father was a white man, and I believe he and my mother loved each other. But so far as I know, I never benefited from it. My mother and my black stepfather worked hard to provide me and my other brothers and sisters with the necessities. If they got any help from my father, I don't know about it. In fact, my light skin has often been a source of derision and discrimination. My life as a black person might have been easier if I had been born darker. When I was a schoolgirl in Millersburg, other children would taunt me and call me half-white. After school I would sometimes have to put down my books and pick up rocks to defend myself on the way home. Then I ran home to escape their rocks and slurs. It was like living in a no-man's-land where I belonged to neither race. Because I was neither completely white or completely black, I've been stigmatized and penalized by both races.

That pattern of discrimination within the black community has continued all my life. It's been a cross I've had to bear. When I took a leave of absence from my work at Mammoth Life and Accident Insurance Company, I expected to get my position back. That was part of the agreement. But the president of the company refused to reinstate me. I don't know why he treated me that way. Maybe he was jealous of me as a woman. Maybe he was jealous of my light skin. Maybe it was a combination of both. All I know is that I was treated unfairly by the company throughout my career with them.

My picture is on the wall at the Kentucky Housing Corporation office in Frankfort to honor me because when I was in the General Assembly I got low-cost housing passed. It was a hard bill to get passed because the Republican governor

Nunn vetoed it, but I kept going back and eventually got it passed. I am proud of that legislation and my part in it. It has helped thousands of low-income families of all races get into decent housing. Wouldn't you expect that people, especially black people, would compliment me for my work? Well, some of them do, but not everyone. One time a black woman said to me, "You're the only black person in Frankfort with a picture on the wall of a public building, and it's because you're light-colored. If you had been as dark as I am, you wouldn't have your picture on that wall." Can you believe that? I've certainly never dealt harshly with my own people because they were lighter or darker than I am. Why should they hold my color against me?

Sometimes it's almost funny the way the subject of my race comes up. One day when I was in the hospital after my stroke, a nurse said, "Mrs. Kidd, are you mixed up?" She was embarrassed because she didn't quite know how to say it. I knew what she meant, but I said, "Mixed up about what, honey?" Another nurse said, "Oh, Mrs. Kidd, what she means is 'Do you have white blood in you?'" I laughed and said, "I think the question is, 'Do you have black blood in you?'" Then I went on and told her I was of mixed blood. She certainly embarrassed herself more than she embarrassed me.

Even people who should know better have questioned my color preference. One afternoon near the end of my lunch break at Mammoth, I was in downtown Louisville on Fourth Street window shopping. I happened to pass two black schoolteachers I knew very well, and I spoke to them. Neither one answered. I was a very sensitive young woman, and their snub hurt me, so I walked up to them and said, "I spoke to you ladies, and you didn't say anything. Didn't you hear me? Is something wrong?" One of them said, almost in a whisper, "Oh, we thought you were passing." I said, "Passing? Passing? Passing for what?" She said, "Oh, you know—passing for white." I said, "Ladies, noooooo, I'm not trying to pass for white. If anything, I've been passing for black all my life because I'm almost 90 percent white." I believe they really thought I was trying to pass for white and that made them angry, and they intentionally snubbed me because they were darker than me. They didn't have the option they assumed I had. It's so very obvious that I'm so much whiter than I am black that I have to pretend to be black. But I can truly say I've never been ashamed of my mother's blood that made me legally a Negro. I loved her so much I didn't care what kind of blood she had or what kind of blood she gave me. I would never have turned my back on my dear mother. I remember an old movie from the fifties called *Imitation of Life*. It's about a young light-skinned woman named Sarah Jane, who rejects her black mother and passes for white. I cannot imagine doing a thing like that to my mother. I'm proud to be who she made me—a person of mixed blood who happens to be mostly white. When people ask me what I am, I say, "American." That's all I need to say.

Traveling with darker friends and family members during the days of segregaton often got me into uncomfortable situations, especially in the South. My first husband did not want me to travel with him on business trips in the South. "You cannot go with me to Birmingham or Atlanta," he'd say, "because I will not allow you to be humiliated by their Jim Crow laws. I don't want any trouble. I don't want a scene." He knew that if I sat with him in the colored section of the train, people would have thought I was a white woman, and that would cause trouble. He certainly didn't want us to split up with me in a white coach and him in a black coach.

I will never forget the incident during World War II when my darker half brother and I were traveling by train from Washington, D.C., to Kentucky to see our parents and the conductor tried to get me to move to the white coach. As I've said, I refused.

"Move? Move to where?" I asked. "Why? Is this seat re-

served?" He said, "Yes, this coach is reserved for colored people.
You'll have to move to another coach. You can't sit here." I
said, "I'm comfortable sitting here. Just let me alone." He said,
"Please move," and walked on off.

In a few minutes the conductor came back a second time
and asked me to leave. I said, "Sir, I am not moving. I am
settled in this seat, so leave me alone." Finally, the conductor
gave up and let me ride in the colored coach.

I was determined not to deny and embarrass my brother
by leaving him alone in the colored coach. He was much
darker than I was, so there was no question about his race. But
he was my brother, and I was not going to leave him. No, I did
not explain to the conductor why I wouldn't move. I didn't
tell him that the black man I was sitting next to was my half
brother and that we were going together to see our family. I
didn't feel that I owed that conductor any sort of explanation.
I just told him I was not going to move. And I didn't.

I was a grown woman. I was wearing my Red Cross uniform. My brother was a grown man wearing his army uniform.
We were a brother and sister going to see our parents before
we shipped out overseas. We were both American citizens serving our country. We didn't owe anybody an explanation.

I've never been bitter about having to live as a legally black
person although I'm over 80 percent white. I've always tried
to live among good and decent people in good neighborhoods.
There are many black neighborhoods I wouldn't want to live
in, and there are many white neighborhoods I wouldn't want
to live in.

Have I ever wished I was 100 percent white? No, I have
not. Life might have been easier for me if I had been all-white
or all-black, but I had to take the color I was given at birth. If I
had tried to live as a white person, I would have been reject-
ing my mother. I could never have done that because I loved
her too much. If my mother had been all-white and I had my
same white father, I would have had no choice. I would have

lived as a white person. My mixed blood has never bothered me personally.

I never tried to be anything I wasn't. I have tried to fulfill my life in trying to be who I am, and that includes the color of my skin.

Last Words

I believe I'm a religious person. I believe firmly in God, and my faith has increased as I've gotten older. But I have my own special understanding of God. I believe that He is everywhere. He's like a giant net or a spider web that covers everything and draws all things together. We don't have to look in special places for Him because He's with us everywhere now. As a Christian, I believe we can seek a special relationship with Him through His only Son, Jesus Christ. When we die, we become one with Him. That is what I think we mean by going to heaven.

I've been going to church all my life, first as a Methodist and now as a member of Plymouth Congregational Church in Louisville. I've studied the Bible and tried to live by the rules of life that it teaches. I attended Woods Chapel Congregational Methodist Episcopal or C.M.E Church in Millersburg when I was a girl. That was my stepfather's church and had a higher level of education than the other black churches. My mother was a member of the Second Christian Church, but while he was alive she went with him to his church. After his death she went back to her own church. Both churches were close to where we lived on Vimont Street. In fact, the C.M.E church, which I joined, was right across the street from our house. One of our ministers was a Mr. Hodges, who was well educated and spoke beautiful English. I don't know whether he had a college degree, but I know he didn't crack any verbs.

I was very active in that church as a girl, especially in church groups like the Epworth League for young people. We had meetings in other little country towns like Georgetown and Winchester and Mt. Sterling, and I was often a delegate to those conferences. It was great fun because we got to stay in the homes of church members, and it was like a great adventure. In the summertime our church would put up a large tent on the church grounds and hold a revival that attracted hundreds of people to every service day and night. The church was a very important part of my growing up years.

When I moved to Louisville I transferred my letter or membership to Brown Memorial C.M.E Church, which was close to where I was living on Chestnut Street. At first I felt comfortable attending the services, and then the pastor started preaching about certain people that everyone knew even though he didn't call their names. That bothered me. But the incident that caused me to leave that church occurred when I was chairman of the hospitality committee and asked the minister if I could speak before the church. He said I could not.

At a later time I asked for permission to speak before the church, and again he denied me. I felt I was being discriminated against because I was a woman. Finally, I said, "You are our pastor, but don't tell me I can't speak to this church because I can and I will. If you don't want to hear me, you can get up and go out. But before you go, I will tell you one thing. I do not come to church on Sunday to hear malicious gossip or to shake hands with the devil. I come here to worship God in a spirit of fellowship. I am tired of hearing you get up and talk about our church members who are good people and doing the best they can." Well, I finally decided to leave that church and join one where I felt I could worship God in spririt and in truth and be appreciated.

That's when I moved to Plymouth Congregational Church, which I still belong to and where I serve on the board of trustees. It has one of the highest levels of education of any church in Louisville, black or white. We have a lot of professional people in our congregation—doctors, lawyers, businesspeople, government workers, but mostly teachers. I have worked long and hard for Plymouth and raised a lot of money to help the church. One Sunday when it was raining, I went to services with a white suit on. Our old roof was made of some kind of metal—maybe copper—but it had rusted, and while I was sitting in my pew, a piece of the roof fell through and hit my suit. I jumped up and said, "Somebody has got to do something about this roof. I will not come to church and have the roof fall in on me." Nobody did anything. When I got home, I said, "Well, if somebody has got to get the ball rolling toward a new roof, it may have to be Mae Street Kidd." So I talked with our pastor and I talked to several men in the church, including Lyman Johnson. I said, "This church is falling apart. It's been a long time since any major maintenance was done on it. I think we should ask each member who can afford it to donate $250 for roof and other repairs the church needs." A few days later I got a letter from Lyman with a check for $250 in it, and he wrote, "I'll give another $250 if you can get at least ten more donations of $250 each." When I read that, I looked up at the ceiling and said, "Lord, You really mean for me to raise this money, don't You?"

The next Sunday I went to church and talked to the pastor, and he said, "Mae, go for it. You're the one to do it." He gave me time to speak to the congregation and present my plan for raising the money to make the repairs. Believe it or not, before the campaign was over, we had raised over $110,000, and all of it came from the church members. You know it made me feel good to lead a successful campaign like that. Through the years I think I've done a lot of good work for my church. Now I'm old and feeble and can't do much for anybody anymore, including myself. But I spend a lot of time thinking over my life and the good things I've tried to do.

I guess I'm like everybody else. Yes, I'd like to be remembered after I'm gone. I'd like for it to be more than a tombstone in a cemetery that sooner or later will break and crumble to dust. I'd like to be remembered for my good deeds for other people. I want people to say that I was a woman of truth and integrity. I never lied or was deceitful, whether I was selling insurance or cosmetics or pushing a bill in the Kentucky legislature. I would like for people to say that I was very sincere and didn't carry on foolishness with anybody. Governor Julian Carroll put it this way one time when he was introducing me. He said, "This lady doesn't play with you, and you don't play with her." I like that because that's the way I tried to be.

I'd like to be remembered as someone who never said she knew everything and didn't argue with people who knew more than she did. But she never had an inferiority complex—never! Perhaps I can say this of myself. Mae Street Kidd was a pretty good gal considering the way she's had to make it. She was a gracious lady who wanted to help other people. She's done a good job with her life. She's a self-made woman. She didn't have a lot of help from a lot of people. If she'd had enough help, who knows what she could have done. She might even have become vice president of the United States! Or governor of Kentucky! Or president of a large company. But Mae Street Kidd did the best she could with the opportunities she had, and she's not ashamed of it. She's not bitter about what life has dealt her. She played the cards that life gave her. She's very proud of her life. She didn't do badly, did she?

Maybe I will be permitted a little vanity now. I've been married twice, but I've always supported myself. I didn't really need either husband. I already had a career when I married the first time. When I was younger, I was a good-looking woman. I've aged a lot since my stroke. I'd like to be remembered for what I was and how I used to look—not what I am now. I don't go around telling my age, but I'm proud that I've lived so long. I don't stand on my doorstep and shout, "Look at me. I'll soon be a hundred years old like my mother." People say, "Ah, come on, Mae, tell us how old you are." I say, "Be patient, honey. Read the obituaries. One of these days you'll find out." I want it to be a big surprise. I want people to say, "Well, I never would have guessed it. She certainly never looked or acted that old."

I'm not worried about where I will be buried. My mother

and father are buried in adjoining cemeteries in Millersburg. He is buried in the white section, along with his wife and one of his daughters and other relatives. He has an impressive monument commemorating his life and achievements. She is buried in the little black cemetery separated from the white cemetery by a rusting barbed wire fence and lies next to her husband and her son by my father. Over her grave is a beautiful maple tree.

Two years ago some friends and I drove to Millersburg for Memorial Day services held in the cemeteries. It was a lovely service. The pastor of my old C.M.E church spoke, and the mayor and many white and black dignitaries were present. After the service we went to my sister's home in Paris, which is about twelve miles south of Millersburg. We had a wonderful dinner, with three kinds of meat and six vegetables. Bourbon County is beautiful any time of the year, but especially in the spring. As we drove south down the pike from Paris to Lexington, it was like driving through Paradise.

In the little Millersburg cemetery, there is room for me close to my mother and near my grandmother, my stepfather, and my older brother and his little girl. She died very young and he had a huge stone of an angel in flight carved for her grave. He was so broken up by her death that he went to the cemetery every day for several years. Now they are all joined in a circle of eternal love. But I'll be a part of it in spirit only because I'll be buried next to my second husband. When you marry, you expect to be buried next to your husband. With two husbands, I had to choose, and I chose to be buried next to James Meredith Kidd. He was an officer during World War II and was therefore eligible to be buried in a national cemetery. It was his wish to be placed in the Zachary Taylor National Cemetery on Brownsboro Road in Louisville. As he lay dying at the Veterans Hospital on Zorn Avenue, I inquired about a lot in the cemetery and was told there were no spaces available. I immediately called Senator Dee Huddleston in Washington and said, "Dee, I need you to pull some strings

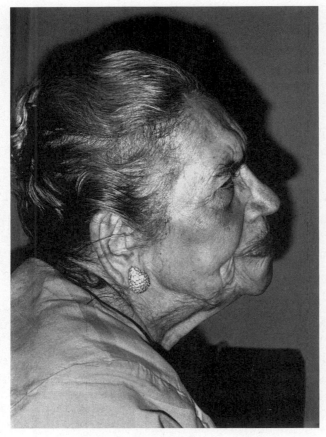

In 1995 at her retirement apartment in Louisville

and get a burial place for my husband, who is on his death-
bed." He said, "I'll see what I can do." It took him less than a
day, and Mr. Kidd is now buried at Zachary Taylor National
Cemetery, where he wanted to be. At one time I thought I
would be buried by my first husband, who rests in Louisville
Cemetery. But I don't like the way that cemetery looks. The
graves there are not well tended. I'll be placed at Zachary Taylor where the graves are kept neat and trimmed. Who knows?
Maybe in time somebody will put up a cross recognizing my
service to my country in the Red Cross during World War II.

Indeed, as my life draws to a close, I would like to be remembered.

Today is such a warm, beautiful day. I know the sun is
shining and the spring flowers are blooming in my yard. I know
the world is putting on its spring show. If I only had my eyesight again, what a time I'd have! I've read in the Bible about
miracles, but I've never known anyone who experienced one.
I've never read in the newspapers about the blind seeing. But
I know miracles can happen and I wish, I wish for a miracle to
restore my sight. I'm trying to accept things as they are. I'm
trying to work with myself, and I ask the Lord to forgive me
for bemoaning my condition. I know He's not pleased with
me for complaining. He has been good to me all my life. He
is still good to me. When I think of where I came from and
how far I went, I know I've done all right.

I hope the Lord can say of me when I'm finished, "Well
done, thou good and faithful servant. Thou hast been faithful
over a few things. Now I will make thee ruler over many things.
Enter thou now into the joy of thy Lord." Oh yes, it has been
beautiful. The Lord has been with me all the days of my life. I
know the sun is shining through my stained glass windows,
and the spirit of the Lord is blessing us all. Smell the peonies
on my hall table. Before you leave, I want you to cut a bou-
quet to take home as a memento of a woman who loves beautiful things and can now enjoy them only in memory.

Epilogue

May 1995. Come in and be seated in my retirement apartment at Treyton Oak Towers. My assistant will get you a glass of iced tea if you want one. I'm doing all right here. I have my privacy. All the medical attention I need is close by. Yes, I had to sell my car and my house. It had to be done. And I didn't cry at all. I'm still trying hard to accept things I can't change. I believe I've made a little progress.

April 1996. I'm not doing very well, Baby Doll, and I had to give up my apartment and move down here to the infirmary. I know the spring flowers are blooming again at my old homeplace, and I miss them so much. But now I can look forward to a place where my sight will be restored and I can see my mother and all my loved ones again. And I can smell the flowers of Paradise forever. And I am not afraid.

Index

190   INDEX

J.O. Blanton House, 130-31
Jackson, Jesse, 142, 159
Jackson, Maynard, 8, 140, 141
Jamaica, 153
Jefferson, Thomas, 147
Jewish Hospital (Louisville), 60,
    159-60, 166
Jews, 60, 159-60
Jim Crow laws (Louisville), 41
Job Corps Center, 34
Johnson, Lyman T., 145, 182
Johnson, Lyndon, 144
Jones, Charles Robert (father), 3,
    4, 15, 27-30, 175, 184
Jones, Christine (niece), 5
Jones, Elizabeth (paternal
    grandmother), 29
Jones, George William (brother),
    5, 26, 27, 28, 30, 31
Jones, Katherine, 5
Jones, Leila MacClintock, 3

Kankakee Shores, Ill., 68
Kennedy, Edward, 120
Kennedy-King Award, 138
Kentucky, 162
Kentucky Children's Home, 33
Kentucky Commission on
    Women, 138
Kentucky Derby, 82-83, 135, 145
Kentucky General Assembly, xi,
    7, 34, 81, 107, 109, 113, 128,
    138, 142, 145, 175
Kentucky Housing Corporation,
    119, 137, 155, 175
Kentucky Human Rights
    Commission, 113
Kentucky Negro Education
    Association, 63-64
Kentucky State University
    (formerly, Kentucky State

College for Negroes), 87, 138,
    139, 158
Kentucky Wesleyan College, 15
Kidd, James Meredith, III, 57, 61,
    68-72, 101, 108-9, 135, 184
Kidd, Mae Street: as an Ameri-
    can, 161-62, 174; career in
    cosmetics, 50, 51-54; career in
    insurance, 34-36, 37-38, 41-51,
    56-59, 132; career in politics,
    107-26, 136; cars, 51-53, 64-66,
    80-81, 90, 93, 173; celebrity
    guests, 81-82; chased by
    German submarine, 96;
    church, 23-24, 38; contribu-
    tions to civil rights, 127-34;
    courtship, 65; discrimination,
    92-93, 98-99, 100, 121, 124,
    129-30, 147, 174-79; divorce,
    71-72; girlhood, 15-36; "good"
    English, 63, 142, 155-56;
    home, 9, 73, 75-81; honors and
    awards, 138-39; husbands, 61-
    72; illnesses, 6-7, 163-71;
    imaginary playmate, 20;
    personal appearance, 11-12, 39,
    56-57, 172, 183; poet, 155-56;
    ratification of 13th, 14th, and
    15th Amendments to U.S.
    Constitution, xii, 124-25; Red
    Cross assistant club director,
    95-101; religious beliefs, 180-
    86; role model, 135-36; rules
    for success, 136-37; scholar-
    ship fund, 74; schooling, 19,
    32-34; sex education, 24;
    1937 flood, 66-67; trips, 42,
    135
King, James, 58
King, Martin Luther, Jr., 138,
    141-42